AN ANTHOLOGY OF SPANISH POETRY
1500–1700

Part I 1500–1580

AN ANTHOLOGY OF SPANISH POETRY 1500–1700

Part I 1500-1580

with notes and introduction

by

ARTHUR TERRY

Professor of Spanish, Queen's University, Belfast

PERGAMON PRESS

OXFORD · LONDON · EDINBURGH · NEW YORK
TORONTO · SYDNEY · PARIS · BRAUNSCHWEIG

Pergamon Press Ltd., Headington Hill Hall, Oxford
4 & 5 Fitzroy Square, London W.1
Pergamon Press (Scotland) Ltd., 2 & 3 Teviot Place, Edinburgh 1
Pergamon Press Inc., Maxwell House, Fairview Park, Elmsford, New York 10523
Pergamon of Canada Ltd., 207 Queen's Quay West, Toronto 1
Pergamon Press (Aust.) Pty. Ltd., 19a Boundary Street,
Rushcutters Bay, Sydney, N.S.W. 2011, Australia
Pergamon Press S.A.R.L., 24 rue des Écoles, Paris 5ᵉ
Vieweg & Sohn GmbH, Burgplatz 1, Braunschweig

First edition 1965
Library of Congress Catalog Card No. 65–22538

*Printed in Great Britain by Blackie & Son Ltd., Glasgow,
reprinted lithographically by Anchor Press, and bound by
Wm. Brendon, both of Tiptree, Essex*

08 011112 2 (flexicover)
08 011113 0 (hard cover)

CONTENTS

		PAGE
Introduction		ix
Note on Versification		xxix
Garci Sánchez de Badajoz (1480?–*post* 1534)		1
1. Recontando a su amiga un sueño que soñó		1
2. Villancico		4
Pedro Manuel Ximénez de Urrea (1486?–1529?)		5
3. Romance		5
4. Villancico		6
Juan Alvarez Gato (*c.* 1440–1509)		8
5. Letra		8
6. Cantar enderezado a Nuestro Señor		9
Fray Ambrosio Montesino (d. 1513?)		10
7. La noche santa		10
Juan del Encina (1468–1529?)		11
8. Villancico		11
9. Villancico		12
10. Romance y villancico		13
Gil Vicente (1465?–1536?)		15
11. Muy graciosa es la doncella		15
12. En la huerta nace la rosa		16
13. Halcón que se atreve		16
14. Dicen que me case yo		17
15. Los amores de la niña		18
16. Vanse mis amores, madre		18
Juan Fernández de Heredia (*c.* 1485–1549)		20
17. Que las manos tengo blandas		20
18. ¡El mi corazón, madre		20
19. Enemiga le soy, madre		21

Cristóbal de Castillejo (1492?–1550)   22

   20. Villancico   23
   21. Canto de Polifemo, traducido de Ovidio   23

Juan Boscán (1474?–1542)   36

   22. A su amiga, enviándole un cancionero de sus coplas   37
   23. Antigua llaga que en mis huesos cría   37
   24. Dulce soñar y dulce congojarme   38
   25. ¡O gran fuerza de amor, que así enflaqueces   38
   26. Como aquel que en soñar gusto recibe   39
   27. Como el patrón que, en golfo navegando   39

Francisco Sá de Miranda (1481–1558)   40

   28. ¡Quién viese aquel día   40
   29. ¡Sola me dejaste   41

Garcilaso de la Vega (1501?–1536)   42

   30. Escrito está en mi alma vuestro gesto   43
   31. A Dafne ya los brazos le crecían   44
   32. En tanto que de rosa y azucena   44
   33. Canción tercera   45
   34. Egloga tercera   47

Diego Hurtado de Mendoza (1503–1575)   59

   35. Redondillas y glosa   59
   36. Nadie fíe en alegría   61
   37. A un retrato   62
   38. Cual simple mariposa vuelve al fuego   62

Sebastián de Horozco (1510?–1580)   63

   39. Sobre la canción vieja y malentendida que dice así: "Señor Gómez Arias . . ."   63

Santa Teresa de Jesús (1515–1582)   65

   40. Véante mis ojos   65

Hernando de Acuña (1518–1580?)   67

   41. Un novillo feroz y un fuerte toro   67
   42. Como vemos que un río mansamente   68

Gutierre de Cetina (1514/17–1554/57)   69

   43. Ojos claros, serenos   69
   44. Por vos ardí, señora, y por vos ardo   70

45. Como garza real, alta en el cielo   70
46. Horas alegres que pasáis volando   71

Gregorio Silvestre (1520–1569)   72
  47. Decid los que tratáis de agricultura   72
  48. La vida se nos pasa, el tiempo vuela   73
  49. Mortales: ¿habéis visto mayor cosa   73

Juan de Timoneda (d. 1583)   75
  50. Soy garridica   75
  51. Tres serranas he encontrado   76

Jorge de Montemayor (1520?–1561)   77
  52. Cántica   78
  53. ¡Sea bienvenido, sea   80

Luis de Camoens (1524–1579)   81
  54. Redondillas   81
  55. Irme quiero, madre   82
  56. El vaso reluciente y cristalino   83

Jerónimo de Lomas Cantoral (c. 1540–1600)   84
  57. Ya de mis quietos días el sereno   84

Fray Luis de León (1527–1591)   85
  58. Vida retirada   86
  59. A Francisco Salinas   89
  60. Noche serena   90
  61. Morada del cielo   93
  62. En la Ascensión   94

Baltasar del Alcázar (1530–1606)   96
  63. Id, suspiros ardientes   96
  64. Rasga la venda y mira lo que haces   97

Fernando de Herrera (1534–1597)   98
  65. Elegía   99
  66. Vuela y cerca la lumbre y no reposa   101
  67. Dulce el fuego de Amor, dulce la pena   102
  68. Alma, que ya en la luz del puro cielo   102
  69. Ahora que cubrió de blanco hielo   103
  70. Amor, en un incendio no acabado   103
  71. Rojo sol, que con llama glorïosa (1578 version)   104

72. Rojo sol, que con hacha luminosa (1582 version) 104
73. Rojo sol, que con hacha luminosa (1619 version) 105
74. Por la pérdida del Rey Don Sebastián 105

Francisco de Figueroa (1536–1617?) 109

75. Partiendo de la luz, donde solía 109
76. Quien ve las blancas y hermosas rosas 110

Francisco de Aldana (1537–1578) 111

77. Mil veces callo que romper deseo 112
78. Reconocimiento de la vanidad del mundo 112
79. Carta del Capitán Francisco de Aldana para Arias Montano sobre la contemplación de Dios y los requisitos della 113

Francisco de la Torre (dates unknown) 126

80. Mira, Filis, furiosa 126
81. Sigo, silencio, tu estrellado manto 127
82. ¡Cuántas veces te me has engalanado 128

Pedro Laynez (c. 1538–1584) 129

83. Salga con la doliente ánima fuera 129
84. Memorias tristes del placer pasado 130

Gaspar Gil Polo (d. 1585) 131

85. Cuando la brava ausencia un alma hiere 131

San Juan de la Cruz (1542–1591) 132

86. Cántico espiritual 134
87. La noche oscura 140
88. Llama de amor viva 142
89. Aunque es de noche 143
90. Tras de un amoroso lance 144
91. El pastorcico 145

Notes to the Poems 147

Glossary 169

Suggestions for Further Reading 171

Index of First Lines 173

INTRODUCTION

I

THIS anthology begins with a few poems written about the year 1500 or, in some cases, slightly earlier. The alternative would have been to start a quarter of a century later, with the introduction of Italianate poetry by Boscán and Garcilaso, but this would have meant an error of perspective. For, although all the major poems of the sixteenth century derive in some way from the Italianate tradition, this was not the only form of poetry available to sixteenth-century writers; and, in a more general sense, it would be wrong to underestimate the extent to which fifteenth-century themes and preoccupations survive into the next century. This, of course, is only one aspect of the process by which the Middle Ages are absorbed by the Renaissance; however original sixteenth-century writers may be in other respects, it is clear that their fundamental ideas on many subjects, from the structure of the universe to the nature of sexual love, were still largely medieval. Conversely, the really revolutionary events of the sixteenth century—the publication of Luther's ninety-five theses in 1517, of Machiavelli's *Prince* in 1532, or of Copernicus' theory of planetary motion in 1543—have little or no effect on the poetry of the time. By the end of the sixteenth century, the general medieval picture of the world which has survived into the Renaissance is beginning to seem precarious; but until then, however much medieval ideas may be simplified or enriched, they are seldom rejected.

All fifteenth-century Spanish poetry is either courtly or popular: both types of poetry are unmistakably medieval, and both retain their significance for the sixteenth century. The love poems of

ix

the fifteenth-century *cancioneros*[1] have their roots in the poetry of
the troubadours, which flourished in Provence from the end of
the eleventh century and later spread over most of Western
Europe. This is a court poetry, based on a conception of love
unknown to antiquity, but which is the origin of what we now
think of as "romantic love". The normal vehicle for such poetry
is allegory, though the type of long allegorical poem represented
in France by the *Roman de la Rose* ceases to be cultivated in Spain
after the fifteenth century. The basic elements of courtly love, on
the other hand, combine easily with certain features of Renaissance
neo-Platonism, and are still recognizable in the seventeenth
century, notably in the love poetry of Quevedo (1580–1645).
C. S. Lewis, whose book *The Allegory of Love* (Oxford, 1936) is still the
best work on the subject, lists the main characteristics of courtly
love as "humility, courtesy, adultery and the religion of love".
The lover is humble because his lady has absolute power over him;
the service he pays her resembles that which a feudal vassal owes
to his lord, and courtly love poetry often adapts the terminology
of feudalism to its own ends. Such love will be a test of the lover's
courtesy, of his ability to behave delicately without hope of reward;
the civilizing influence of courtly love lies in its appeal to dignity
and self-sacrifice. Nevertheless, the two remaining characteristics
may seem to cancel out any ennobling effects obtained by the
others: for courtly love can only exist outside the marriage bond—
the lady the poet addresses is usually another man's wife—and it
is blasphemous in that the lover claims to worship the God of
Love rather than the God of Christianity. Yet, in Lewis's words,
"any idealization of sexual love, in a society where marriage is
purely utilitarian, must begin by being an idealization of adultery".
If such love is immoral, it is also true that medieval theology re-
gards all passion as sinful; the inevitable result is a division between
Church and Court of which the courtly love poets were fully
aware. The obvious expression of this antagonism is the concep-
tion of love as a substitute-religion, one in which not only love

---

[1] The term *cancionero* means "song-book", but many of these collections also
contained longer moral or allegorical poems for reading only.

itself but also the poet's lady, may be given divine status. But if some poets appear to dwell deliberately on the antagonistic aspect, many come to regard the love-religion as a truancy from Christian beliefs, as something to be renounced in the course of time. Though the fusion of sexual love and religious experience which Dante achieves in the *Divine Comedy* is unique, there are dozens of poets, even in the sixteenth century, who dismiss their love poems as part of the errors of youth.

The first important collection of courtly love poetry in Castile appears in the *Cancionero de Baena* (c. 1445). By this time, the themes and subject-matter of the Provençal tradition have been successfully transferred to Castilian, and the characteristic stress on artistry and verse-technique is firmly established. This achievement is sustained and consolidated during the second half of the fifteenth century. There are no striking innovations in later *cancionero* poetry, but there are a number of interesting shifts in emphasis, among them the increasing use of fixed forms like the *villancico* and the *canción*, and a tendency for love poetry to centre on extreme, and often neurotic, situations. In many poems of the period, the lover's suffering becomes the desire for a death which, paradoxically, is his one hope of life, the "morir para no morir" which was to be taken up in a mystical sense by Santa Teresa de Jesús in the next century. This condition of emotional instability is deliberately invited; in the words of Pedro Salinas: "la vida es vivida en un estado de desequilibrio sentimental, equilibrado por la voluntad poética, que lo quiere así, y lo cultiva como tema". In such situations, the poet's aim is to assert his powers of endurance—in a phrase of the time, "experimentarse en fortaleza". His sincerity, or lack of it, is scarcely considered; his function is to appear as a representative of true love, rather than as an actual lover. In all this, there is an element of ritual play which links *cancionero* poetry to other types of court ceremonial, and this is also reflected in the complex verbal artifice which is worked to death by its less talented practitioners. Nevertheless, it represents a kind of verse which, for all its dependence on abstractions, paradox and word-play, keeps alive a tradition which underlies some of the finest poetry of the sixteenth and seventeenth centuries. However much the Italianate poets refine on this tradition by incorporating neo-Platonic concepts or by direct study of Petrarch, their treatment of love is largely inherited from the fifteenth century.

Popular poetry is significantly omitted from the *Cancionero de Baena*. Though many of the finest ballads and popular lyrics were in existence by 1450, it was some time before they were granted serious literary status. The revaluation of popular poetry is one of the most striking changes which take place in the late fifteenth century; its course can be gauged by comparing the curt dismissal of the ballads or *romances* by the Marqués de Santillana (1398–1458) —"estos romances y cantares de que las gentes de baja y servil condición se alegran"—with Nebrija's acceptance of the *romance* as a literary model in his *Gramática castellana* (1492). Serious appreciation of the *romance* in court circles begins under Enrique IV of Castile (1454–1474) and gains rapidly with the musicians of the court of the Catholic Kings. Several of the best poets writing in 1500 were also musicians: Encina, for example, set a great deal of popular poetry to music, and one of his own *romances* is included in the anthology (p. 13). This revival is also linked to the early progress of humanism in the Peninsula: Nebrija is only one of a number of scholars and writers whose interest in the national past leads them to a revaluation of popular art and beliefs. (Another instance of this is the respect shown for popular sayings or *refranes* in the serious literature of the time, as, for example, in the *Diálogo de la lengua* of Juan de Valdés, written in 1535–6.)

Even so, the traditional ballad or *romance viejo* falls largely outside this anthology. The finest examples date from well before 1500, and there is a falling-off, both in quantity and quality, after 1525. This decline in actual composition, however, comes at a time when existing ballads are at the height of their popularity. Menéndez Pidal, the greatest authority on the Spanish ballad, places this period between 1515 and 1580. Before this, its status is still a little uncertain: the poets and musicians of the late fifteenth century, including Encina, seem to have mistrusted the metrical freedom of the *romance viejo*; their own ballads use full rhyme, not assonance, and this is the only type which is seriously considered in Encina's *Arte de poesía castellana* (1496). The most influential anthology of the time, the *Cancionero general* of Hernando de Castillo (1490–1511), also shows a guarded attitude to the *romance*, only admitting those which have been glossed by more recent poets. This state of affairs is reflected in other collections printed during the first half of the sixteenth century; it is not until the publication of the *Cancionero de romances* (Antwerp, *c.* 1547–9) that an entire volume is given to ballads. This is the climax of the fashion, and by this time the ballad has been taken up by the musicians of the court of Charles V. One of the greatest of the sixteenth-century *vihuelistas*[1], Juan Vásquez, published his musical settings of *villancicos (Recopilación de sonetos y villancicos)* in 1551, two or three years after the appearance of the *Cancionero de romances*, and eight years after the *Obras* of Boscán and Garcilaso (1543), the first great land-mark of the new Italianate poetry. These three works represent the three most vigorous possibilities open to Spanish poets about the year 1550. The *romance* remains something of which every sixteenth-century poet is conscious, even though the composition of new *romances viejos* ceases. As Pidal says: "Los más grandes poetas de la nación tienen en su memoria las viejas creaciones roman-císticas, y las tienen recibidas por tradición oral, no aprendidas en la lectura de cancioneros impresos." The proof of this comes in the second half of the sixteenth century, with the appearance of the *romance nuevo*, the conscious imitation of the traditional ballad, which is to achieve a new kind of artistic success after 1580 in the work of Góngora and Lope de Vega.

The vogue of the popular lyric runs parallel to that of the *romance*, with one striking difference, namely, that once it achieves literary status at the end of the fifteenth century, it continues to be imitated by all kinds of poets for almost 150 years. The vitality of *poesía de tipo tradicional*, as it is generally known by Spanish scholars,

---

[1] The *vihuela* is an instrument strung and played like the lute, but with a body resembling that of the guitar. It was the most serious solo instrument used at the Spanish court during the sixteenth century.

remains almost constant from the earliest medieval lyrics until its decline in the second quarter of the seventeenth century. This astonishing continuity is partly a question of verse-structure: the essential nucleus of Spanish popular poetry is the short stanza-form known as the *villancico*, which originates in the Mozarabic poetry of the eleventh century. Though the individual pattern may vary, the typical form of a popular lyric in Castilian consists of an opening *villancico* which is glossed in a number of separate stanzas, each with a refrain or *estribillo* based on the original *villancico*. (See, for example, the poem by Encina beginning "No te tardes que me muero . . .", p. 12.) This is clearly a musical form, and the fortunes of the popular lyric, like those of the *romance*, are closely linked to the revival of court music under the Catholic Kings and to the achievement of the sixteenth-century *vihuelistas*. Neither kind of poetry is represented in the *Cancionero de Baena*; the *villancico* makes a first, brief appearance in the *Cancionero de Herberay* (post 1458), and is taken up on a large scale by the dramatists of the early sixteenth century: Encina, Lucas Fernández and, above all, Gil Vicente. At roughly the same time, the *Cancionero general* of 1511 includes a number of *villancicos* by courtly poets like Garci Sánchez de Badajoz, some of which become widely-known in the course of the sixteenth century. Nevertheless, there is a difference between the *villancicos* of the later *cancionero* poets, which make use of courtly love material, and the more traditional re-creations of a Gil Vicente or a Lope de Vega. One striking aspect of the development of traditional poetry in the sixteenth century is the number of *villancicos* written in Castilian by Portuguese poets: among others, by Gil Vicente, Sá de Miranda and Camoens. The *villancico*, in fact, like the short metres of the *cancioneros*, continues to flourish long after Italianate poetry has become the dominant mode, and many poets in the second half of the sixteenth century move freely from one style to the other.

By the end of the fifteenth century, the practice of glossing older poems is applied to both secular and religious lyrics. In this last form, the *glosa* becomes part of the general current of *poesía. a lo divino* which enjoys a considerable vogue until well into the seventeenth century. The *versión a lo divino* or *contrafactum*,[1] to use the term suggested by Professor Wardropper, is normally a short poem whose original secular words have been revised so as to give them a spiritual meaning. (Thus, Santa Teresa's poem beginning "Véante mis ojos, / dulce Jesús bueno . . ." is an *a lo divino* version of an older love poem: "Véante mis ojos / y muérame yo luego . . .".) Most *contrafacta* were intended to be sung to popular tunes; the only exceptions were those based on the work of sophisticated poets like Petrarch and Garcilaso. This type of poetry is not confined to Spain, but represents a practice which stretches from early Christian times to the modern negro spiritual. Its practitioners often have little poetic talent, and the results are usually mediocre. In Spain, this is certainly true of the learned imitations of Boscán and Garcilaso, but many of the sacred versions of popular poetry, from Fray Ambrosio Montesino and Encina to Gregorio Silvestre and Santa Teresa, remain fresh and memorable. Compared with the religious verse of a Luis de León or a San Juan de la Cruz, such poetry is bound to appear superficial. The *a lo divino* poet, however talented, is almost always an elaborator rather than a creator, and at the worst his work is merely parasitic. Unlike the serious religious poet, he is never writing directly from religious experience; his aim is simply to instruct and to edify by presenting the outward signs of spiritual belief in an easily palatable form. (The one notable exception to this tendency is San Juan de la Cruz's poem *El pastorcico*. See p. 145 and notes.) Despite this, it would be wrong to ignore the existence of a strong current of devotional poetry which, like the *romance*, though inferior to it in quality, was familiar to a great many people in the sixteenth century who knew nothing of the Italianate tradition.

II

Cultural relations between Spain and Italy, never very close during the Middle Ages, enter a new phase in the early fifteenth

---

[1] The term is based on phases like "villancico contrahecho (i.e. 'counterfeited') a lo divino" often found in early collections.

century, leading to the conquest of Naples by Alfonso V of Aragon in 1443. Even so, it was more than eighty years before Italian poetry became a serious literary influence in Spain: the handful of sonnets written by the Marqués de Santillana remained an isolated example among the prevailing *cancionero* poetry. The real change came swiftly and dramatically in the 1520s, first in the work of Boscán and, shortly afterwards, in the early verse of Garcilaso de la Vega, the first great poet of the Spanish Renaissance. The initial impulse came from the meeting which took place in 1525 between Boscán and the Italian diplomat Navagiero, who suggested that Boscán— already an established poet in the *cancionero* manner—should attempt to write "sonetos y otras artes de trobas usadas por los buenos autores de Italia". Boscán was well aware of the technical difficulties involved: 'Y así comencé a tentar este género de verso, en el cual al principio hallé alguna dificultad por ser muy artificioso y tener muchas particularidades diferentes del nuestro", and he goes on to imply that only the friendly competition of Garcilaso made him persevere in his experiments. Two things should be noticed at this point: one is that the Italian influence on Spanish poetry was virtually inevitable at this period, and would have come about in any case through Garcilaso's own contacts with Italy a few years later; the other is that Italian poetry itself had reached a crucial point in the 1520s. The important figure here is Pietro Bembo, a minor poet and an influential literary theorist, who in 1525 published his *Prose della Volgar Lingua*, one of the decisive critical documents of the Italian Renaissance. In these dialogues on literary taste, Bembo sets out to establish the Tuscan writers of the fourteenth century, and in particular Petrarch, as the models for correct literary usage in Italian, and at the same time claims that the chief object of vernacular writers should be to imitate the achievement of classical Greek and Latin literature. The second proposal embodies one of the great commonplaces of Renaissance theory; the first is the more original, in that it overlooks the far greater genius of Dante, and sets up Petrarch as the chief model for a new kind of fine writing. Some of Bembo's detailed arguments apply mainly to the literary possibilities of Italian, but his choice of

Petrarch as the master of poetic style and his concentration on the qualities of the Petrarchan love-sonnet have much wider consequences. In point of time, Spain is the first country outside Italy to feel the influence of this new literary programme. Boscán and Garcilaso begin their study of Italian poetry only a short time after the publication of Bembo's treatise, and their own work shows most of the characteristics assoociated with the Italianate (or Petrarchan) tradition.

Many of these characteristics are concerned with the formal nature of verse: here the most obvious innovation is the establishment of the hendecasyllable, or 11-syllable line, as the standard unit of serious poetry, in contrast to the shorter lines (particularly the octosyllable) used in the lyric poetry of the *cancioneros*. In addition, a number of individual verse-forms and types of poem are adopted from Italian: *terza rima*, *ottava rima*, the *lira*,[1] the sonnet, the Petrarchan ode, and other longer forms, including the pastoral eclogue, the elegy and the verse-letter. The Italian influence also brings with it a close interest in classical models, especially the poetry of Virgil, Horace and Ovid, and there is a striking increase in allusions to classical myth from Garcilaso onwards. All these features are easily identified; there are, however, more generalized influences which are just as important: the increasing use of philosophical concepts derived from Renaissance neo-Platonism and, above all, the contact with the body of poetic theory which began to shape itself in the 1530s and 40s around the early translations and commentaries of Aristotle.

Sixteenth-century poetic theory is an international phenomenon which springs partly from Renaissance humanism and partly from the spread of the Italianate tradition itself. In Spain, the most interesting discussions of the nature of poetry do not appear until the last quarter of the sixteenth century. Nevertheless, sixteenth-century poetry and poetic theory form such a coherent unity that any poem written in the Italianate tradition is a concrete embodiment of the theory which lies behind it, and even a slight working

---

[1] The *lira* is the Spanish name for a stanza-form first used in Italian. See Note on Versification.

knowledge of this can add unsuspected dimensions to the poetry. The first thing to be said is that the assumptions on which any Renaissance poem is written differ considerably from those held by any poet or reader of the last 150 years. This is easier to understand once one realizes that all Renaissance theory and practice depends in the first instance on a philosophical basis—more precisely, on a view of reality and of the nature of the universe which has far more in common with medieval views on Man's place in the Divine Order than with the theories of a Descartes or a Newton. Broadly speaking, the Renaissance still retains the idea of a hierarchical cosmos in which the universal and the particular are inextricably bound together by a complex network of correspondences. Or, to use a favourite concept of neo-Platonism, the relation of earth to heaven can be expressed as that of a "microcosm" to a "macrocosm"—of a "little world" to a greater—with the corollary that earthly objects are finite expressions of divine archetypes. (See, for example, Luis de León, *Noche serena*, ll. 36–40, where heaven is described as

> . . . aqueste gran trasunto,
> do vive mejorado
> lo que es, lo que será, lo que ha pasado.)

It is this view of reality which underlies Renaissance opinions on the purpose of poetry; it also determines some of its basic literary conceptions like imitation and the theory of styles, and colours the whole nature of its poetic imagery.

For any Renaissance poet, the short answer to the question "what is poetry for?" lay in Horace's phrase "prodesse et delectare": poetry should give both profit and pleasure. No modern reader would disagree with the second of these requirements, though he might be surprised by some of the types of pleasure which sixteenth-century critics commend. The first notion is more difficult to accept, since it seems to imply that poetry "teaches", that it has an openly didactic purpose, in which pleasure will merely act as the bait. In fact, however, the didactic purpose of Renaissance poetry works much more subtly than this. It is noticeable, for example, how much theorists are concerned, not only with the purpose of poetry in general, but with the purpose of the individual poem, and with the way in which this will determine its structure and language. This is why, where a modern critic will often point to the way in which a poem has been shaped by the writer's experience, a Renaissance critic will speak of a poem's "cause", meaning both the subject of the poem and the poet's intention in writing it. Thus, to take a concrete example, the *subject* of Garcilaso's Third Eclogue (as stated in ll. 52–6) is the behaviour of a group of nymphs in a pastoral setting. The pastoral convention imposes certain conditions which determine the imagery and diction of the poem; but, conversely, it is these conditions which enable Garcilaso to achieve his *intention* by incorporating the theme of personal loss in an objective work of art. In general terms, the intention becomes much more important, both in the conception of the poem and in its final evaluation by the critic. No Renaissance poet would find this unnatural: he would fully expect his poem to be judged in terms of the truth it conveyed, and of the effect which his presentation would be likely to have on a reader's mind.

Inevitably, a poetry which claims to be expressing truth in this way will be dealing with concepts rather than with emotional states; it will accept all the help which logic and rhetoric can give it, and it will not feel plain statement to be "unpoetic". On the other hand, it will not exclude the expression of emotional power, since it recognizes that emotions play a vital part in human action. Nor will it succumb to another danger which might seem implicit in a didactic theory: that of reducing the poem to its "message", i.e. to those ideas which can be taken out and paraphrased. Here, in fact, the second half of the "prodesse et dilectare" formula acts as a check on the first: if part of a poem's aim is to teach, then the reader will be more powerfully convinced by the truths it conveys if he can find pleasure in the relation between words and subject. This idea of a just relationship between the form and content of a poem is included in what is probably the key-term in Renaissance literary theory: the concept of decorum. Decorum, the sense of what is fitting in a given context, is the guiding principle from

which most other sixteenth-century critical notions take their
standards. It is, of course, just the kind of literary principle we
would expect to find in a society which believes that everything in
the universe has its divinely-appointed place. In practice, it is
responsible for many kinds of critical decision, from choice of
genre to the use of individual words and images. Moreover, it is
decorum which qualifies the didactic theory of poetry as the
Renaissance understood it, so that writing a poem will not be
merely a question of conveying ideas, but of clothing them in a
proper aesthetic form.

This question of the poet's "truthfulness" involves another of
the basic concepts of Renaissance theory, that of imitation. The
term is used by sixteenth-century critics in several different, but
related, senses: (i) imitation of older writers, classical or vernacular,
in order to perfect one's own literary style; (ii) the Aristotelian
concept of drama as the "imitation of an action"; and (iii) the
idea that the artist "imitates" nature. Renaissance non-dramatic
poetry is concerned with the first and third senses, and it is the
third which needs some explanation. To begin with, we must
discard the idea that poetry should be an accurate transcript of
reality. Though Renaissance poets often use sensuous imagery in
their poems, they are seldom, if ever, concerned with the precise
copying of objects which we expect from a representational
painter. Renaissance description is never "realistic" in this sense.
Even when Aldana opens one of the most remarkable descriptions
in sixteenth-century poetry (*Carta para Arias Montano*, ll. 352–432)
with the words "quiero el lugar pintar . . .", the minute observa-
tion of the natural scene which follows is interspersed with phrases
like "altas y ponderadas maravillas" . . . "de varia operación, de
varia empresa", so that even a factual detail like "*retorcidas* caracoles"
(l. 382) conveys the beholder's amazement at the richness and
variety of Creation. What matters, in other words, is not so much
the precision of the individual details as the way in which these
are related to the wider, more conceptual, meaning of the poem.

The theoretical justification for such a technique lies in the
acceptance of Aristotle's distinction between poetry and history:

history deals with the local and the particular, poetry (in the sense of all imaginative writing) with the ideal and the universal. In more concrete terms, the historian will be concerned with the character of a particular king, the imaginative writer with the ideal nature of kingship, "the king, not as he was, but as he should have been". Nor must we think of the poet as someone who imposes order on a chaotic nature. Nature, for the Renaissance, is never chaotic: however inscrutable she may seem to human understanding, she is still the source of all forms, including the form in which the poet expresses the substance of his poem. The artist's task, therefore, is to co-operate with nature, in order to reveal truths which might otherwise remain hidden. If we look for the qualities which sixteenth-century theorists demand of a successful "imitation", we find that they are normally of three kinds, each of which is expected to assist the other: (i) the images of a poem will be "artificial", not in the modern, derogatory sense, but to the extent that they contribute to the formal excellence of the poem, to its value as an artistic construction; (ii) they must also be chosen so as to help the poet in his *ordering* of nature: the success of his interpretation will be judged by its coherence, and individual images considered in terms of their appropriateness to the poem's basic purpose; (iii) they must, in addition, assist in the stating of truth, not merely the creation of orderly patterns, as in (ii), but of concepts and values which may be discussed intellectually. The idea of imitation is present in all three stages: in (i), the artist is acting as nature herself often does—as a craftsman who produces an artifact (see Garcilaso, Third Eclogue, ll. 57–64); in (ii), he is imitating a pattern which lies beneath the surface of nature, and in (iii), he is conveying the truth which such a pattern embodies.

The character of the "imitation", though not the general principle, will vary according to the seriousness and scope of the poem. These are matters which also depend on the idea of decorum, and it is decorum which is responsible for the Renaissance theory of styles. The connection is made clear in a statement like the following, from the late sixteenth-century theorist Luis

Alfonso de Carvallo: "Decoro es una decencia y una consideración que se ha de tener a toda la obra, y a cada parte de ella, a las personas, cosas y palabras . . . (Se guarda el decoro) considerando la materia de que se ha de hacer, si es humilde, y común, como cosas para reir y donaire, o si es mediana como en algunos sucesos ordinarios de personas de mediano estado, o si es materia alta, como heroicos hechos, o levantados conceptos y pensamientos, o de cosas divinas y sagradas y conforme fuese aplicable el estilo, humilde . . . mediano y grave" (*Cisne de Apolo*, 1602). This division into three styles—the low or "base", the "mean", and the high or "elevated"—applied, with some variation, to individual types of writing or genres. Thus, the epic, as the highest form of non-dramatic verse known to antiquity, demands the elevated style (a fact which helps to account for the sixteenth-century revival of literary epic); the mean (or middle) style includes the more serious kinds of lyric poetry, while the base style is suited to satire and poetry dealing with humble people and situations. Sixteenth-century theory goes further than this, in fact, and a work like Herrera's commentary on Garcilaso (1580) gives detailed definitions of the main types of Italianate poem—the sonnet, the eclogue, the ode and the elegy—with observations on the kind of imagery and vocabulary which may be used in each. Theorists often differ as to the strictness with which such divisions are to be observed—the the mean style is sometimes praised because it is able to incorporate images from both the elevated and the base styles—but, generally speaking, a particular type of poem is taken as belonging to one or other of the three styles, and the poet must observe decorum by choosing his images accordingly. What one finds, therefore, is not the idea of a single style suitable for poetry, a universal "poetic diction", but that of a number of styles suited to a variety of poetic subjects. This may even help to account for the ease with which Spanish poets, even after 1550, are able to alternate between the Italianate and the *cancionero* traditions. Certainly, the division of styles is much more than a literary artifice, and the terms themselves—high, mean and low—suggest the basic levels of a hierarchical society.

All the aspects of Renaissance theory so far mentioned come together in the functioning of poetic imagery. In any sixteenth-century poem based on the Italianate tradition, the nature of the images is determined by the poet's intention and by his ability to apply the concept of imitation. Because poetry is more concerned with the universal than with the particular, images and epithets are used to direct the reader's mind towards the value of what is being described, rather than to its precise physical appearance. (See the comment above (p. xx) on the lines from Aldana's *Carta para Arias Montano.*) This is why an image must always be considered in its poetic context; what in itself may seem a straightforward piece of description will more often than not take on an evaluative function when seen as part of a whole poem. If it does not, it is irrelevant, and no sixteenth-century theorist would hesitate to condemn it. This is easy enough to recognize in poems which praise physical beauty. No one could mistake lines like

> con voz, que entre las perlas blanda suena,
> teñido en puro ardor de fresca rosa . . .
>
> (Herrera, *Elegía*, ll. 25-6)

for literal description; there is no attempt at sensuous accuracy, and the evaluation is enforced by the use of "perlas" and "rosa". A modern reader is more likely to have difficulty with descriptions contained in poems which use pastoral or mythological conventions. Yet, if we are tempted to condemn pastoral poetry as a means of escaping from reality, it is worth remembering that no sixteenth-century poet ever thought of it in this way. It is an axiom of Renaissance theory that the pastoral functions on two levels: that the pastoral situation is never described for its own sake, but is a means of presenting general moral situations and solutions, that, as one Elizabethan theorist puts it: "under the veil of homely persons, and in rude speeches . . . (poets may) insinuate and glance at greater matters". Similarly with myth: if a modern reader is inclined to read a mythological poem as plain narrative, or to regard classical allusions as mere displays of erudition, he should bear in mind that for a Renaissance writer mythological images had fixed significances, that allusions to Icarus or Midas, for example, were economical ways of referring to temerity or greed which an educated reader would immediately recognize. On a more ambitious scale, myth is often used metaphorically as a means of discussing live issues; when this happens, descriptive language will almost inevitably take on further meanings. The most striking example of this occurs in a seventeenth-century poem—Góngora's *Fábula de Polifemo y Galatea* (1613)—but some of the possibilities of the method are already inherent in Garcilaso's Third Eclogue, where a number of well-known myths are made to reflect on the poet's attitude to his own suffering.

The use of metaphor in Renaissance poetry is never felt to conflict with the use of non-figurative language, since both can serve equally well to convey universal significances. Three reasons are usually given by the theorists for the importance of metaphor: it adds variety; it is "necessary" because sometimes there are no words for naming things, and it makes for intellectual richness by widening the area of meaning. As usual in Renaissance theory, all three qualities invoke either the reader's pleasure or his judgement: if a metaphor sharpens the meaning of a poem or states a just affinity between different objects, then it is to be praised; if it is far-fetched or confused (i.e. if it is neither clear nor truthful), it has failed in its purpose. Sixteenth-century critics do not deny that a metaphor may appeal to the senses; this is part of the force of metaphor. Where they differ from modern critics is in not looking to metaphor for a more *accurate* rendering of a sense-impression. Here again, one is made to feel the connection between poetry and logic: what really matters is the relationship which the poet establishes between the terms of his comparison, rather than the nature of the terms themselves. The actual relationship may appear apt, witty or profound; the point is that it will have linked two different things on the basis of a universal quality which they share. Thus, in the lines from Herrera quoted above, the replacement of "dientes" by "perlas" creates only a very imprecise sense-impression; the metaphor is justified principally by the abstract qualities which link the two terms: beauty, value and perfection.

Any brief summary of Renaissance poetic aims runs the risk of making them sound more consistent than they actually were. In practice, poets and critics *did* disagree over literary models, over vocabulary or over the boundary between difficulty and obscurity. Nevertheless, the amount of agreement over fundamental questions is impressive, as is the degree of coherence between theory and practice. For a modern reader, of course, understanding of the problems is no guarantee that he will enjoy the solutions, that is to say, the poems themselves. Fortunately, most sixteenth-century poems still speak for themselves, in some cases magnificently; yet even some of the best modern critics have shown that it is possible to misunderstand such poems by failing to recognize the assumptions which governed their writing. Clearly, it would be a mistake, even if it were possible, to attempt to respond to a poem as a sixteenth-century reader would have done; every reader belongs to his own time, and historical criticism can never take the place of first-hand literary judgement. Yet it would be equally wrong to approach a Renaissance poet with the kind of expectations appropriate to a Romantic or a Symbolist writer, though of all errors this is the most difficult for a twentieth-century reader to avoid, since his own preconceptions of poetry are most likely to be based on the poetic tendencies of the last 150 years. The best one can do, therefore, is to aim at what one scholar has called a "working contemporaneity" with older poetry, a compromise which at least reduces the risk of false interpretations. Even a little knowledge of Renaissance literary theory can sharpen one's appreciation of the poetry and help to explain some of its most lasting qualities. If nothing else, the theory reminds us of the profound seriousness with which sixteenth-century writers worked; without the theory, and deprived of the resources of logic and rhetoric, the poetry would have been infinitely less rich.

III

This anthology shows how Italianate poetry developed in Spain between Garcilaso and Herrera. The process is swift and intense: Garcilaso gives an impulse to the poetry of his time which can still be felt in the next century. His influence on the love poetry of the following generations is enormous, yet never tyrannical: poets like Cetina, Acuña and Silvestre have their own distinctive voices, and with Herrera the movement towards a different, more complex, type of writing is becoming increasingly clear. The Italianate forms also have an important effect on the religious verse of the time: the *lira*, which Garcilaso uses in a single poem, becomes the principal stanza-form in the poetry of Luis de León and in the Carmelite tradition which leads to San Juan de la Cruz, while the humanistic spirit of devotion combines with another verse-form, *terza rima*, to produce one of the most remarkable poems of the sixteenth century, the *Carta para Arias Montano* of Francisco de Aldana.

With a few exceptions, the poems contained in this volume were written before 1580. This is a crucial year in several ways: it sees the publication of Herrera's monumental text of Garcilaso, the commentary to which looks back over the development of Italianate verse since the 1530s and, at the same time, establishes poetic standards for the future; it is also the date of the earliest poems of Góngora, the outstanding lyric poet of the next generation; and it marks the birth of another great poet, Quevedo, who with Góngora, carries both the Italianate and the popular traditions to their furthest point of development in the first half of the seventeenth century. Looking ahead a little, one could add that in 1582 Herrera, the last and most dedicated of the sixteenth-century Petrarchan poets, published the only collection of his poems to appear in his lifetime, and possibly wrote no more new poems after this date. And only a few years later, the first plays of Lope de Vega mark the beginning of a great revival of verse drama which will inevitably have its effect on lyric poetry.

IV

Finally, a word about the methods used in making this anthology. I have avoided fragments on principle, in the belief that critical reading has more chance of success with whole poems. This has, however, meant excluding one important branch of sixteenth-century poetry, the literary epic; fortunately, the interested reader may refer to Professor F. W. Pierce's excellent anthology, *The Heroic Poem of the Spanish Golden Age* (Dolphin, Oxford, 1947). I have also excluded passages from verse drama, except for a number of songs from the plays of Gil Vicente; here again, the test, as also in the case of the poem taken from Gil Polo's novel *La Diana enamorada*, was that the poems should be self-contained.

The introductory notes to each poet are intended to combine the most important biographical facts with a brief critical "placing" and a reference to the best, or most accessible, modern edition. The notes to the poems are mainly concerned with points of interpretation and with allusions which may be unfamiliar to modern readers. Difficult passages are sometimes paraphrased in English, at other times in Spanish—whichever seemed to bring out the meaning of the original more clearly. The final glossary contains only words and forms which would not normally appear in a good modern Spanish–English dictionary.

The spelling of the texts has been modernized, except where this would involve a change of pronunciation. Thus, *dixo* becomes *dijo*,[1]

---

[1] This is a difficult case. Two changes are at work throughout the period of these poems: one of pronunciation and one of spelling. Pronunciation of -x- (= English *sh*) continues into the seventeenth century (*Quixote* becomes French *Quichotte* shortly after 1605). But the change of this sound to Modern Spanish *jota* had already begun in many areas and is almost universal after 1630. This was also the sound whch developed during the sixteenth century from the -j- (as in French *jardin*) found in words like *hijo*, whose spelling was imitated in the development of words originally written with -x-. The change in spelling from *dixo* to *dijo* occurs over the same period as the change in sound, but does not exactly parallel it. Thus we find in different texts, authors and areas examples of *dijo* with the old pronunciation and *dixo* with the new, as well as many more cases which cannot be resolved. To save the reader the embarrassment of all these confusions, I have opted for -j- throughout and left the question of pronunciation open.

conoscer/conosçer become *conocer*, and *estraño* is printed as *extraño*. Contractions like *dello(s)*, *della(s)*, *desto(s)* and *desta(s)* are retained, as is the infinitive + object pronoun construction *vendello* = *venderlo* etc., since they are often rhymed with words like *bello(s)*, *puesto(s)*, *puesta(s)*. A certain amount of modernization seems legitimate, and even essential, in an anthology which is intended for both sixth-form and university students, and those who require a more scholarly text may refer to some of the editions listed in the notes. Readers should, however, be warned that sixteenth-century spelling is by no means consistent, and that even the best modern editions of sixteenth-century poets vary a good deal in the criteria they adopt. Most people who have studied sixteenth-century poetry in early editions would probably agree that something of a poem's flavour is lost when its spelling and punctuation are modernized,[1] yet this seems a small price to pay compared with the gain in clarity.

By modern standards, sixteenth-century writers and printers tended to overpunctuate, and occasionally I have revised the punctuation of a poem where the meaning seemed to demand it. Clearly, these are compromises, but I feel that any other solution would have placed unnecessary obstacles in the way of readers, many of whom may be approaching Renaissance poetry for the first time.

In conclusion, I should like to thank those friends who have helped me with advice and encouragement at various stages in the making of this anthology, especially Professor A. A. Parker, Professor E. L. Rivers, Mr N. G. Round and Mr D. G. Rowlands.

---

[1] For example, the first four lines of the Herrera sonnet on p. 102 read as follows in the 1619 edition:

> Dulce'l fuego d'Amor, dulce la pena,
> i dulce de mi daño es la memoria,
> cuando renueva Amor l'antigua istoria,
> qu'a su grave tormento me condena.

NOTE ON VERSIFICATION

Spanish metres are classified according to the number of syllables in the line. The most common metres in this period are the hendecasyllable *(endecasílabo)*, the octosyllable *(octosílabo)*, the heptasyllable *(heptasílabo)* and the hexasyllable *(hexasílabo)*. These lengths are calculated on the basis of a line ending in a stressed syllable followed by a single unstressed syllable. Thus, a standard hendecasyllable (or 11-syllable) line will run:

$$\text{re|no|var | el | pla|cer | o | la | tris|tu|ra}$$
$$1 \quad 2 \quad 3 \quad\ 4 \quad\ 5 \quad 6 \quad 7 \quad 8 \quad\ 9 \ 10 \ 11$$

Two variations are possible: a line may end in a stressed syllable:

$$\text{A|mor, | a|mor, | un | há|bi|to | ves|tí}$$
$$1 \quad\ 2 \quad\ 3 \quad\ 4 \quad\ \ 5 \quad\ 6\ 7\ 8 \quad\ 9\ 10$$

or in two unstressed syllables:

$$\text{De | dos | ár|bo|les | al|tos | la | col|gá|ba|mos}$$
$$1 \quad\ 2 \quad\ 3\ 4\ 5 \quad 6\ 7 \quad 8 \quad 9\ 10\ 11\ 12$$

Both these lines are hendecasyllables; the decisive factor is that the final stress falls on the tenth syllable.

If two vowels come together, either within a single word, or at the end of one word and at the beginning of the next, they are normally slurred and count as a single syllable:

$$\text{pre|so‿y | for|za|do‿y | so|lo‿en | tie|rra‿a|je|na}$$
$$1 \quad 2 \qquad 3 \quad 4 \quad\ 5 \qquad 6 \quad\ 7 \qquad 8 \quad\ 9 \quad\ 10\ 11$$

(Mute *h*, with rare exceptions, does not prevent this:

$$\text{que | jun|tos | tan|tos | ma|les | me‿han | lle|va|do)}$$
$$1 \quad\ 2\ \ 3 \quad 4\ \ 5 \quad 6\ \ 7 \qquad 8 \qquad 9\ 10\ 11$$

Hiatus of vowels is rare in Spanish poetry after 1450, except in

xxix

words where it normally occurs, such as *río, hastío, vendía*. In other cases it is sometimes indicated by the use of a diaresis (e.g. *süave*).

The following are the chief verse-forms represented in the anthology:

canción: (i) In the second half of the fifteenth century, the term *canción* is applied to any kind of courtly poem which is meant to be sung. (ii) In the poetry of the Italianate tradition, the *canción* is the Spanish equivalent of the *canzone* or Petrarchan ode. The verse-form used in the *canción* is a variable combination of 11- and 7-syllable lines, ranging in length from the *lira* to the 20-line stanzas of Garcilaso's *Canción IVa*. In any single *canción*, the pattern fixed in the opening stanza is repeated throughout the poem. The stanza is often constructed in two parts, the first consisting entirely of hendecasyllables, with the shorter line(s) occurring in the second part, or forming a transition between the two, as in Herrera's ode *Por la pérdida del Rey Don Sebastián*. The same type of stanza is also used in the pastoral eclogue from Garcilaso onwards.

canción paralelística: a form used originally in the Galician-Portuguese *cantares de amigo* of the thirteenth century. In adapting it to Castilian, Gil Vicente adds the initial *estribillo* characteristic of the *villancico* and prefers the octosyllabic metre. The *estribillo* is developed in short stanzas (often couplets), each of which closely reflects the sense and syntactical pattern of the previous one. See Gil Vicente, "Muy graciosa es la doncella".

cuarteto: a quatrain, or group of four hendecasyllables, rhyming ABAB or ABBA. See San Juan de la Cruz, *El pastorcico*.

estribillo: a short group of lines (usually two, three or four) which forms the starting-point for a *villancico* or *zéjel* and is repeated, as a whole or in part, at the end of each stanza.

glosa: a poem consisting of an initial theme and a series of stanzas which comment on it and repeat its lines one by one. The commonest type of *glosa* consists of an opening *redondilla*, followed by four stanzas of ten lines or less, each of which incorporates a line of the *redondilla*. See Hurtado de Mendoza, "Va y viene mi pensamiento".

lira: the Spanish name for the 5-line stanza-form which Garcilaso imitated from the Italian poet Bernardo Tasso (1493–1569) and used in the *Canción Va*, which begins "Si de mi baja *lira* . . .". It is one of a number of stanza-forms used by Tasso to reproduce the effect of a Horatian ode; it consists of a combination of 11- and 7-syllable lines $(7 + 11 + 7 + 7 + 11)$, rhyming aBabB. In this form, it is used by many later sixteenth-century poets, including Luis de León and San Juan de la Cruz, though its popularity declines after 1580. San Juan's *Llama de amor viva* uses a 6-line variation of the *lira*, rhyming abCabC.

madrigal: a short composition in the Italianate manner, intended for musical performance and consisting of a free combination of 11- and 7-syllable lines. See Cetina, "Ojos claros, serenos" and Baltasar del Alcázar, "Id, suspiros ardientes".

octava rima, octava real (ottava rima): a stanza formed by eight hendecasyllables, rhyming ABABABCC, first used in Spanish by Boscán and shortly afterwards by Garcilaso in his *Égloga tercera*. Later it becomes the standard vehicle for the literary epic and other types of narrative poem.

quintilla: a stanza of five octosyllabic (or shorter) lines, containing two rhymes which may be combined in a number of different ways: ABABA, ABBAB, ABAAB etc. In *cancionero* poetry two *quintillas* are often combined to form a 10-line stanza; see Garci Sánchez, "La mucha tristeza mía"; Boscán, "Ahí van las ansias mías". Castillejo often uses a variant of the *quintilla* known as the *quintilla con quebrado inicial*, in which each stanza opens with a half-line of four syllables. Such poems normally begin with a *redondilla*, which is followed by a series of *quintillas:* ABBA (*redondilla*): cCDDC —eEFFE . . . etc., as in the *Canto de Polifemo*.

redondilla: a stanza consisting of four octosyllabic (or shorter) lines, rhyming ABAB or ABBA. See Hurtado de Mendoza, "Va y viene mi pensamiento". In the second half of the sixteenth century the term came to be applied to longer stanzas, which were known as *redondillas de cinco (siete, ocho,* etc.) *versos.* See Camoens, "De dentro tengo mi mal", which uses a 7-line pattern with an *estribillo.*

romance: Spanish ballads are composed of a series of octosyllables, in which the odd-numbered lines are unrhymed and the even-numbered ones are rhymed in assonance. The same assonance is used throughout the poem; some ballads written about 1500 use full rhyme instead of assonance (see Introduction).

soneto: The sonnets of Boscán and Garcilaso are modelled on those of Petrarch, and their example is followed by all subsequent sixteenth-century poets. The fourteen hendecasyllablic lines are composed of two quatrains + two tercets. The rhyme-scheme of the quatrains—ABBA: ABBA—remains constant throughout the period. That of the tercets varies: Garcilaso and Herrera have a preference for CDE: CDE, Cetina for CDE: EDC, and few poets confine themselves to a single combination.

terceto (terza rima): a group of three hendecasyllables, repeated in series with interlocking rhymes: ABA: BCB: CDC etc. See Herrera, *Elegía*; Aldana, *Carta para Arias Montano*.

villancico: a traditional song-pattern, normally in 8- or 6-syllable lines. It consists of an *estribillo*, or theme-stanza, of two to four lines, which is developed in a series of longer stanzas (often *redondillas*,) each of which leads back into the original *estribillo*, or a part of it. The term *villancico* is sometimes applied to the *estribillo* itself.

zéjel: a metrical form of Mozarabic origin, similar to the *villancico*, but distinguished by its central unit of three lines with identical rhyme, followed by a fourth line which rhymes with the *estribillo*: AA *(estribillo)*: BBBA: AA (repetition of *estribillo*). This basic pattern admits of a number of variations, principally in the length of the *estribillo*, which is not always repeated in full. See Encina, "Ojos garzos ha la niña", "No te tardes que me muero"; Gil Vicente, "Los amores de la niña", "Muy graciosa es la doncella". (This last poem combines the *zéjel* with the technique of the *canión paralelística*.) Sebastián de Horozco's poem *La niña de Gómez Arias*, though usually printed, as here, in hexasyllables, is really a *zéjel* whose lines have been divided into half-lines: "mı-vi *(estribillo)*: trajistes-vendistes-hecistes: merceí" (return to *estribillo*).

GARCI SÁNCHEZ DE BADAJOZ
(1480? – *post* 1534)

DESPITE his surname, Garci Sánchez was probably born at Écija, in
Andalusia. In his lifetime he was famous as a court wit and a
musician. His eventual insanity and death as the result of an
unhappy love-affair caught the imagination of his contemporaries.
His poems figure prominently in the *Cancionero general* of 1511 and
in subsequent sixteenth-century collections and were praised
by later poets, among them Herrera and Lope de Vega. They
represent most of the major kinds of *cancionero* poetry, including
allegory *(Infierno de Amor)* and religious parody *(Liciones de Job)*. "La
mucha tristeza mía", the finest of Garci Sánchez's shorter poems,
shows a skilful use of earlier medieval topics (dream, symbolic
birds, the God of Love) within the framework of a personal lyric.
Texts in P. Gallagher, *The Life and Works of Garci Sánchez de Badajoz*,
Támesis, London, 1968.

1

RECONTANDO A SU AMIGA UN SUEÑO QUE SOÑÓ

La mucha tristeza mía
que causó vuestro deseo,
ni de noche ni de día,
cuando estoy donde no os veo,
no olvida mi compañía.
Yo los días no los vivo,
velo las noches cativo,
y si alguna noche duermo,
suéñome muerto en un yermo
10 en la forma que aquí escribo.

Yo soñaba que me iba
desesperado de amor
por una montaña esquiva
donde si no un ruiseñor
no hallé otra cosa viva.
Y del dolor que levaba,
soñaba que me finaba,
y el Amor que lo sabía,
y que a buscarme venía
20   y al ruiseñor preguntaba:
     —"Dime, lindo ruiseñor,
¿viste por aquí perdido
un muy leal amador
que de mí viene herido?"—
—"¿Cómo? ¿Sois vos el Amor?"—
—"Sí, yo soy a quien seguís,
y por quien dulces vevís
todos los que bien amáis."—
—"Ya sé por quién preguntáis,
30   por Garci-Sánchez decís.
     Muy poco ha que pasó
solo por esta ribera,
y como le vi y me vio,
yo quise saber quién era
y él luego me lo contó
diciendo:—"Yo soy aquel
a quien más fue Amor crüel,
crüel que causó el dolor,
que a mí no me mató amor,
40   sino la tristeza de él."
     Yo le dije:—"¿Si podré
a tu mal dar algún medio?"
Díjome:—"No, y el porqué
es porque aborrí el remedio
cuando de él desesperé."
Y estas palabras diciendo

　　y las lágrimas corriendo,
　　se fue con dolores graves,
　　yo con otras muchas aves
50　fuemos en pos de él siguiendo,
　　　hasta que muerto cayó
　　allí entre unas acequias,
　　y aquellas aves y yo
　　le cantamos las obsequias,
　　porque de amores murió:
　　y aun no medio fallecido,
　　la tristeza y el olvido
　　le enterraron de crüeles,
　　y en estos verdes laureles
60　fue su cuerpo convertido.
　　　De allí nos quedó costumbre
　　las aves enamoradas
　　de cantar sobre su cumbre
　　las tardes, las alboradas,
　　cantares de dulcedumbre."
　　—"Pues yo os otorgo indulgencia
　　de las penas que el ausencia
　　os dará, amor y tristura,
　　a quien más su sepoltura
70　servirá con reverencia"—.
　　　Vime alegre, vime ufano
　　de estar con tan dulce gente,
　　vime con bien soberano
　　enterrado honradamente
　　y muerto de vuestra mano.
　　Allí, estando en tal concierto,
　　creyendo que era muy cierto
　　que veía lo que escribo,
　　recordé y halléme vivo,
80　de la cual causa soy muerto.

2

VILLANCICO

Secáronme los pesares
los ojos y el corazón,
que no pueden llorar, non.
   Los pesares me secaron
el corazón y los ojos,
y a mis lágrimas y enojos,
y a mi salud acabaron.
Muerto en vida me dejaron,
traspasado de pasión,
10 que non puedo llorar, non.
   Y de estar mortificado
mi corazón de pesar,
ya no está para llorar,
sino para ser llorado:
ésta es la causa, cuitado,
ésta es la triste ocasión,
que non puedo llorar, non.
   Al principio de mi mal
lloraba mi perdimiento,
20 mas agora ya estó tal
que de muerto no lo siento;
para tener sentimiento
tanta tengo de razón,
que non puedo llorar, non.

PEDRO MANUEL XIMÉNEZ DE URREA
(1486?–1529?)

XIMÉNEZ DE URREA was an Aragonese nobleman, the second son of the Conde de Aranda. He is the only Aragonese poet of any distinction in this period. His *Cancionero* (1513) contains imitations of Petrarch and Encina, as well as a remarkable verse-rendering of Act I of *La Celestina;* his best work, however, is in the form of *villancicos* and *romances*. The two poems I have included show a natural feeling for popular poetry, and also a sharp eye for detail. The second is an attractive, if outspoken, variation on the theme of *la bella mal maridada*. *Cancionero*, ed. Villar, Saragossa 1878.

3

ROMANCE

En el placiente verano,
do son los días mayores,
acabaron mis placeres,
comenzaron mis dolores.
Cuando la tierra da hierba
y los árboles dan flores;
cuando aves hacen nidos
y cantan los ruiseñores;
cuando en la mar sosegada
10   entran los navegadores,
cuando los lirios y rosas
nos dan los buenos olores;
y cuando toda la gente,
ocupados de calores,
van aliviando la ropa

y buscando los frescores;
do son las mejores horas
las noches y los albores,
en este tiempo que digo
20 comenzaron mis amores
de una dama que yo vi,
dama de tantos primores:
de cuantos es conocida,
de tantos tiene loores.
Su gracia por hermosura,
tiene tantos servidores
cuanto yo por desdichado
tengo penas y dolores;
donde se me otorga muerte
30 y se me niegan favores.
Mas yo nunca olvidaré
estos amargos dulzores,
porque en la mucha firmeza
se muestran los amadores.

4

VILLANCICO

Madre, cuando enviudaré
a Zaragoza me iré.
Allí las viudas holgadas,
mucho más que las casadas,
allí son visitadas
de los que les tienen fe.
Visitadas y queridas,
muy queridas y servidas,
servidas y bien sabidas,
10 que yo sé bien cómo fue.
Viuda huelga en Zaragoza
más que casada ni moza;
cada cual dellas retoza

 con mil cosillas que sé.
  Madre, aquellas son mujeres
 que, con sus dulces aferes,
 ellas dan muchos placeres
 y tienen quien gelos dé.
  ¡Oh si viese ya morir
20 a mi marido, por ir
 donde sé que he de sentir
 placer con amor que habré!
  Si mucho el vivir le dura
 yo le daré gran tristura,
 que por ir donde hay holgura
 la vida le quitaré.

JUAN ALVAREZ GATO
(*c.* 1440–1509)

JUAN ALVAREZ GATO was probably born in Madrid. Most of his life was spent at the Castilian court, where he was *mayordomo* under Queen Isabella. As a young man, he wrote love poems and exchanged verse-letters with Gómez Manrique and other poets; later, he was one of the first poets to compose religious lyrics on popular models. Both the poems which follow are of this type. The first is the more successful rhythmically; the second is a good example of what his most recent editor calls "su devoción de hombre que se dirige a Dios como se podría dirigir a un amigo, con cortesía y respeto,... con unción religiosa y afectividad devota". *Obras completas*, ed. J. Artiles, Madrid, 1928.

5

LETRA

Venida es, venida
al mundo la vida.
　Venida es al suelo
la gracia del cielo
a darnos consuelo
y gloria complida.
　Nacido ha en Belén
el que es nuestro bien:
venido es en quien
10　por él fue escogida.
　En un portalejo
con pobre aparejo
servido de un viejo

su guarda escogida.
  La piedra preciosa,
ni la fresca rosa,
non es tan hermosa
como la parida.

6

CANTAR ENDEREZADO A NUESTRO SEÑOR

  Amor, no me dejes,
que me moriré.
  Que en ti só yo vivo,
sin ti só cativo;
si me eres esquivo
perdido seré.
  Si mal no me viene,
por ti se detiene;
en ti me sostiene
10 tu gracia y mi fe.
  Que el que en ti se ceba,
que truene, que llueva,
no espera ya nueva
que pena le dé.
  Que aquel que tú tienes
los males son bienes,
a él vas y vienes
y muy cierto lo sé.
  Amor, no me dejes,
20 que me moriré.

FRAY AMBROSIO MONTESINO
(d. 1513?)

Fray Ambrosio Montesino was a Franciscan monk, attached to the monastery of San Juan de Reyes in Toledo; shortly before his death he was appointed Bishop of Sarde, in Albania. He was an excellent prose-writer and translator of devotional works. His *Cancionero* (1508) is dedicated to Ferdinand of Aragon; it contains a number of fine religious lyrics, often embedded in longer poems. Among his contemporaries, only Gil Vicente equals the vivid simplicity with which he re-creates traditional models. *Cancionero*, in *Biblioteca de autores españoles*, vol. 35, Madrid, 1925, pp. 401–66.

7

LA NOCHE SANTA

No la debemos dormir
la noche santa,
no la debemos dormir.
   La Virgen a solas piensa
qué hará
cuando al Rey de luz inmensa
parirá,
si de su divina esencia temblará,
o qué le podrá decir.
10   No la debemos dormir
la noche santa,
no la debemos dormir.

JUAN DEL ENCINA
(1468–1529?)

Juan del Encina is best known as an outstanding dramatist and musician. His early life was centred on Salamanca, where he may have studied under the humanist Antonio de Nebrija. His earliest dramatic pieces were performed in the household of the Duque de Alba. Much of Encina's life was spent in minor ecclesiastical posts in Spain and Italy, where he was a protégé of the Papal court. He was not ordained until 1519; in the same year he made a pilgrimage to Jerusalem, a journey recorded in his long poem, *La Trivagia*. His *Cancionero* (1496) contains an *Arte de poesía castellana*, one of the earliest statements on poetry by a Spanish writer, and an interesting free adaptation of the *Bucolics* of Virgil. His best poems are those which use popular forms; many of them have survived with his own musical accompaniments. Encina's comment on this type of poetry—"pues si bien es mirado: no menos ingenio requieren las cosas pastoriles que las otras mas antes yo creo que más"—is a useful corrective to critics who speak of its "artless spontaneity". *Cancionero* (1496), facsimile ed., Madrid, 1928.

8

VILLANCICO

Ojos garzos ha la niña:
¿quién ge los namoraría?
  Son tan bellos y tan vivos,
que a todos tienen cativos;
mas muéstralos tan esquivos
que roban ell alegría.

Roban el placer y gloria,
los sentidos y memoria:
de todos llevan vitoria
10   con su gentil galanía.
  Con su gentil gentileza
ponen fe con más firmeza,
hacen vivir en tristeza
al que alegre ser solía.
  No hay ninguno que los vea,
que su cativo no sea:
todo el mundo los desea
contemplar de noche y día.

9

VILLANCICO

  No te tardes que me muero,
carcelero,
no te tardes que me muero.
  Apresura tu venida
porque no pierda la vida,
que la fe no está perdida.
Carcelero,
no te tardes que me muero.
  Bien sabes que la tardanza
10   trae gran desconfianza;
ven y cumple mi esperanza.
Carcelero,
no te tardes que me muero.
  Sácame desta cadena,
que recibo muy gran pena,
pues tu tardar me condena.
Carcelero,
no te tardes que me muero.
  La primer vez que me viste

20   sin te vencer me venciste;
       suéltame pues me prendiste.
     Carcelero,
     no te tardes que me muero.
         La llave para soltarme
       ha de ser galardonarme,
       proponiendo no olvidarme.
     Carcelero,
     no te tardes que me muero.
         Y siempre cuanto vivieres
30   haré lo que tú quisieres,
       si merced hacerme quieres.
     Carcelero,
     no te tardes que me muero.

10

ROMANCE Y VILLANCICO

     Por unos puertos arriba
   de montaña muy escura
   caminaba un caballero
   lastimado de tristura:
   el caballo deja muerto,
   y él a pie por su ventura,
   andando de sierra en sierra
   de camino no se cura.
   Huyendo de las florestas,
10   huyendo de la frescura,
   métese de mata en mata
   por la mayor espesura.
   Las manos lleva añudadas,
   de luto la vestidura,
   los ojos puestos en tierra
   sospirando sin mesura;
   en sus lágrimas bañado,
   más que mortal su figura;

su beber y su comer
20 es de lloro y amargura,
que de noche ni de día
nunca duerme ni asegura,
despedido de su amiga
por su más que desventura.
A haberle de consolar
no basta seso y cordura:
viviendo penada vida,
más penada la procura,
que los corazones tristes
30 quieren más menos holgura.

—"¿Quién te trajo, caballero,
por esta montaña escura?"
—"¡Ay, pastor, que mi ventura!"

GIL VICENTE
(1465?–1536?)

Gil Vicente was Portuguese by birth. As well as a dramatist of genius—he is the greatest figure in the Peninsular theatre before Lope de Vega—he was a talented musician and a professional silversmith. Of his forty-two surviving plays, only seven are written entirely in Portuguese; many of them contain short lyrics which have rarely been equalled in Spanish at any period. It is likely that some of these poems were collected by Gil Vicente from popular sources; others may be improvisations on existing models. Whatever the truth, their extraordinary richness and variety is beyond dispute, and, unlike his Castilian contemporaries, Gil Vicente is able to draw on the long tradition of the Galician-Portuguese lyric. Dámaso Alonso's judgement underlines the unrepeatable quality of his work: "aunque en el mismo umbral de nuestro Renacimiento, nos ofrece una poesía variada, colorida, humana y divina al mismo tiempo, fuera, muy lejos de los cánones que petrarquismo u horacianismo iban a imponer al Siglo de Oro". Gil Vicente wrote no verse apart from his plays; of the poems included here, only "Muy graciosa es la doncella" is known to be completely original. *Obra lírica castellana*, ed. Dámaso Alonso, *Cruz y raya*, vol. 10, Madrid, 1934, pp. 113–56; 2nd ed., Mexico, 1940.

11

Muy graciosa es la doncella,
¡cómo es bella y hermosa!
Digas tú, el marinero
que en las naves vivías,

si la nave o la vela o la estrella
es tan bella.
    Digas tú, el caballero
que las armas vestías,
si el caballo o las armas o la guerra
10 es tan bella.
    Digas tú, el pastorcico
que el ganadico guardas,
si el ganado o los valles o la sierra
es tan bella.

12

    En la huerta nace la rosa:
quiérome ir allá
por mirar al ruiseñor
cómo cantaba.
    Por las riberas del río
limones coge la virgo:
quiérome ir allá
por mirar al ruiseñor
 cómo cantaba.
10   Limones cogía la virgo
para dar al su amigo:
quiérome ir allá
para ver al ruiseñor
cómo cantaba.
    Para dar al su amigo
en un sombrero de sirgo:
quiérome ir allá
para ver al ruiseñor
cómo cantaba.

13

    Halcón que se atreve
con garza guerrera,

peligros espera.
   Halcón que se vuela
con garza a porfía,
cazarla quería
y no la recela.
Mas quien no se vela
de garza guerrera,
10 peligros espera.
   La caza de amor
es de altanería:
trabajos de día,
de noche dolor.
Halcón cazador
con garza tan fiera,
peligros espera.

14

   Dicen que me case yo:
no quiero marido, no.
   Más quiero vivir segura
nesta sierra a mi soltura,
que no estar en ventura
si casaré bien o no.
Dicen que me case yo:
no quiero marido, no.
   Madre, no seré casada
10 por no ver vida cansada
o quizá mal empleada
la gracia que Dios me dio.
Dicen que me case yo:
no quiero marido, no.
   No será ni es nacido
tal para ser mi marido;
y pues que tengo sabido

que la flor yo me la só,
dicen que me case yo:
20   no quiero marido, no.

15

Los amores de la niña
que tan lindos ojos ha,
que tan lindos ojos ha,
¡ay Dios, quién los haberá!,
¡ay Dios, quién los haberá!
Tiene los ojos de azor,
hermosos como la flor;
quien los sirviere de amor
no sé cómo vivirá,
10   que tan lindos ojos ha.
¡Ay Dios, quién los servirá!
¡Ay Dios, quién los habera!
Sus ojos son naturales
de las águilas reales,
los vivos hacen mortales,
los muertos suspiran allá,
que tan lindos ojos ha.
¡Ay Dios, quién los servirá!
¡Ay Dios, quién los haberá!

16

Vanse mis amores, madre,
luengas tierras van morar.
Yo no los puedo olvidar.
¿Quién me los hará tornar?
¿Quién me los hará tornar?
Yo soñara, madre, un sueño
que me dio en el corazón:
que se iban los mis amores
a las islas de la mar.

10 Yo no los puedo olvidar.
¿Quién me los hará tornar?
¿Quién me los hará tornar?
   Yo soñara, madre, un sueño
que me dio en el corazón:
que se iban los mis amores
a las tierras de Aragón.
Allá se van a morar.
Yo no los puedo olvidar.
¿Quién me los hará tornar?
20 ¿Quién me los hará tornar?

JUAN FERNÁNDEZ DE HEREDIA
(c. 1485–1549)

JUAN FERNÁNDEZ DE HEREDIA is one of the earliest and most attractive
of the Valencian dramatists. He was a protégé of Germaine de
Foix, before whom his *Coloquio de las damas valencianas* was presented
in 1524. Sixteen of his poems appear in the *Cancionero general* of 1511;
his complete works include three dramatic dialogues, some fairly
undistinguished burlesque and devotional verse, and a number of
excellent *villancicos*. Though most of his poems are written in
Castilian, Juan Fernández is one of the last poets to use Valencian
as a literary language. *Obras*, ed. R. Ferreres, *Clásicos castellanos*, vol.
139, Madrid, 1955.

17

Que las manos tengo blandas
de broslar:
no nací para segar.
  ¡Oh manos mías tan bellas,
no para segar nacidas,
si ya no fuesen las vidas
de cuantos osaren vellas!
Sí, para cegar son ellas
en mirar,
10 pero no para segar.

18

¡El mi corazón, madre,
que robado me lo hane!
  No digo que me ha dolido,

antes si me le quería
volver, no le tomaría,
tan bien empleado ha sido.
Quiera Dios, ya que es perdido
el mío, que el suyo gane:
que robado me lo hane.

19

Enemiga le soy, madre,
a aquel caballero yo,
mal enemiga le só.
En quererme es él de sí
tan enemigo cruel,
como yo enemiga de él
por ser amiga de mí.
Nunca en cosa pidió "sí",
que no le dijese "no":
10 tan enemiga le só.

CRISTÓBAL DE CASTILLEJO
(1492?–1550)

Cristóbal de Castillejo was born in Ciudad Rodrigo. He served as a page at the court of Ferdinand and Isabella and later entered the Cistercian order. In 1525 he became secretary to the Archduke Ferdinand, *Rey de Romanos*, and later ruler of Bohemia and Hungary. This part of his life was spent mostly in Vienna, where he died. Castillejo consistently opposed the Italianizing tendencies of Boscán and Garcilaso; the fact that this was a losing battle has tended to obscure the very real qualities of his own poetry. Basically, he is a Renaissance poet who continues to write in *cancionero* metres. His *Canto de Polifemo* is the only successful long poem of the period written outside the Italianate tradition; its freshness and vitality—and, above all, its sustained assurance—are unlike anything to be found in the *cancioneros*. Castillejo's technique of "translation" consists largely of expanding the simple comparisons of the original to include the rich pastoral detail which is one of the poem's chief attractions. In the words of the most recent editor of the poem: "Castillejo no puede concebir a este Cíclope ovidiano sin hacerlo pastor y ganadero a la castellana, y sus palabras se legitiman por su castiza castellanía". The result is a poem which exists in its own right alongside the later, more complex, versions of Carrillo and Góngora. *Obras*, ed. J. Domínguez Bordona, *Clásicos castellanos*, vols. 72, 79, 88, 91, Madrid, 1927–8. *Fábula de Polifemo*, ed. J. F. Montesinos, *Cruz y raya*, Madrid, 1935.

20

VILLANCICO

No pueden dormir mis ojos,
no pueden dormir.

Pero, ¿cómo dormirán
cercados en derredor
de soldados de dolor,
que siempre en armas están?
Los combates que les dan,
no los pudiendo sufrir,
no pueden dormir.

10   Alguna vez, de cansados
del angustia y del tormento,
se duermen que no lo siento,
que los hallo trasportados;
pero los sueños pesados
no les quieren consentir
que puedan dormir.

Mas ya que duerman un poco,
están tan desvanecidos,
que ellos quedan aturdidos,
20   yo poco menos de loco;
y si los muevo y provoco
con cerrar y con abrir,
no pueden dormir.

21

CANTO DE POLIFEMO, TRADUCIDO DE OVIDIO

Hola, gentil Galatea,
más alba, linda, aguileña
que la hoja del alheña,
que como nieve blanquea;

más florida
que el prado verde, y crecida
mucho más, y bien dispuesta,
que el olmo de la floresta
de la más alta medida;
10   más fulgente,
que el vidro resplandeciente;
más lozana que el cabrito
delicado, ternecito,
retozador, diligente;
más polida,
lampiña, limpia, bruñida
que conchas de la marina,
fregadas de la contina
marea, nunca rendida;
20   gracia y brío
agradable al gusto mío,
y del sabor dulce y tierno,
más que soles del ivierno
y que sombra del estío;
en color
muy más noble, y en olor,
que manzanas del labrado,
más vistosa que el preciado
alto plátano mayor.
30   En blancura
más reluciente y más pura
que el hielo claro, lustrosa;
más dulce que la sabrosa
moscatel uva madura
delicada,
y blanca, siendo tocada,
más que la pluma sotil
del blanco cisne gentil
y que la leche cuajada;
40   y aún diría,

si no huyes a porfía,
como sueles, desdeñosa,
que eres más fresca y hermosa
que la huerta regadía.
Sus, pues ea,
tú, la mesma Galatea,
más feroz que los novillos
no domados y bravillos,
que nunca vieron aldea
50 par a par;
muy más dura de domar
que la encina envejecida,
más falaz y retorcida
que las ondas de la mar,
más doblada,
con el salce comparada,
que sus varas delicadas
y que las vides delgadas,
no sufridoras de nada;
60 y a mi ver,
muy más dura de mover
que estas peñas do me crío,
furiosa más que el río
a todo todo correr;
más señora
soberbia, desdeñadora,
que el pavo siendo alabado,
más fuerte que el fuego airado,
en que me quemas agora.
70 Desmedida,
más áspera y desabrida
que los abrojos do quiera,
más cruel que la más fiera
osa terrible parida;
más callada
y sorda, siendo llamada,

que este mar de soledad;
muy más sin piedad
que la serpiente pisada
80   de accidente.
Y lo que principalmente,
si pudiese, te querría
quitar de tu compañía,
es, que eres, no solamente
toda vía
en huir menos tardía
que el ciervo con sus oídos,
despertado a los ladridos
de la clara vocería
90   tras la tela;
más aun, porque más duela
tu huirme en mis tormentos,
más ligera que los vientos
y más que el aire que vuela.
Pero si
tuvieses ya desde aquí
la noticia que debrías,
sé que te arrepentirías
de andar huyendo de mí,
100   y sin verme,
te pesara de perderme,
haciendo de ti mudanza,
y culpando tu tardanza,
trabajaras de tenerme;
porque tengo
cuevas donde agora vengo,
hechas en la peña viva,
sobre que gran parte estriba
de aqueste monte tan luengo;
110   en las cuales
no se sienten las señales
del sol en medio la siesta,

ni el ivierno las molesta
con sus tristes temporales.
Tengo más:
manzanas cuantas querrás,
que hacen doblar las ramas,
de las cuales, si me amas,
a tu placer comerás
120 cuando quieras;
y uvas de dos maneras
en sus parras de contino;
las unas como oro fino,
sabrosas y comederas,
si las vi,
y otras como carmesí,
que son en extremo bellas:
estas, señora, y aquellas
guardo todas para ti.
130 Con tu mano
tú misma, tarde y temprano,
cogerás las blandas fresas
en las selvas y dehesas,
a la sombra en el verano
cada mes;
y en el otoño después
las cerezas montesinas,
y no solamente endrinas,
morenas por el envés
140 y de fuera,
mas también otra manera
de ciruelas generosas,
amarillas y hermosas,
de color de nueva cera.
Si me oyeres,
y por marido tuvieres,
no te faltarán castañas
por estas frescas montañas,

y madroñas, si los quieres,
150   en gran vicio:
que, pues servirte codicio
con todo cuanto hay acá,
cuantos árboles habrá
estarán a tu servicio
y señorío.
Todo este ganado es mío
cuanto miras, si me escuchas,
con otras ovejas muchas,
que andan como de baldío
160   por los valles;
yo te prometo que halles
otras muchas no sé dónde,
que la silva las asconde,
y en los establos y calles
de las cuevas;
tantas son, que si me pruebas
y pides dellas razón
para decir cuántas son,
no sabré dar dello nuevas
170   ni recado;
que nunca las he contado,
ni visto tan mala ves;
que de pobres hombres es
poder contar su ganado.
Pues contarte
loores, parte por parte,
de aquestas ovejas mías
no debo, porque podrías
pensar que hablo con arte
180   falsamente.
Para que más te contente,
no quiero que a mí me creas:
mas que tú mesma las veas.
Cuando estuvieres presente

podrás ver
que apenas pueden mover
las piernas esparnancadas
con las tetas retesadas,
que más no pueden caber.
190 Por tal vía
hay también la nueva cría
en tibios apriscaderos,
tanta copia de carneros,
que decirla no sabría.
Tal y tal,
de tiempo y edad igual,
en otros apriscos tales,
hay cabritos recentales,
regocijado animal.
200 Y de aquí
viene, que acerca de mí
hay leche continamente
blanca, fresca y excelente,
que me sobra por allí;
de la cual
una parte en especial
se guarda para beber;
la otra para hacer
queso, que es lo principal.
210 Item más,
que no sólo gozarás
destos deleites ligeros
y destos dones caseros
y comunes, que ternás
infinitos,
sino de otros exquisitos
que menos veces gozamos,
como son liebres y gamos,
gamuzas y pajaritos
220 muy continos.

Cualque par de palominos
en su tiempo señalado,
y cualque nido tomado
de la cumbre de los pinos.
Dos ositos
hermanos mielgos, chiquitos,
que pueden jugar contigo;
los cuales traje conmigo,
y he hallado muy bonitos;
230   ambos ellos
tan semejantes y bellos
en lo menos y en lo más,
que apenas conocerás
la diferencia de entre ellos,
porque engaña;
hijos de una muy extraña
osa, vellosa y escura.
Hallélos en la espesura
de la más alta montaña,
240   do ella mora;
y en viéndoles a deshora,
que de ti se me acordó,
dije: "¡Oh! Questos quiero yo
guardar para mi señora".
Sus pues ya,
vuelve tus ojos acá,
tu voluntad endereza;
saca tu linda cabeza
de la mar adonde está,
250   con que pones
mi vida en estas pasiones.
Ven ya, Galatea, ven;
no me trates con desdén
ni menosprecies mis dones;
que yo sé
que tú no tienes por qué

me menosprecies así;
que yo me conozco a mí.
Y ha poco que me miré
260 a ventura,
para ver mi hermosura,
y me vi en el agua clara
todo mi cuerpo y mi cara,
y me plugo mi figura.
Mira, amor,
mi persona en derredor,
cuán grande soy desde el suelo,
que Júpiter en el cielo
no será cierto mayor;
270 porque vos
soléis contar entre nos
un Júpiter, no sé cuál
reinar como principal
y más poderoso dios.
Pues con esto,
mira, señora, de presto
encima de mi estatura
la muy gran cabelladura
que cuelga sobre mi gesto
280 denodado,
y al uno y al otro lado
por los hombros se levanta,
y les hace sombra tanta
como un bosque muy cerrado.
Ni se vea,
que porque mi cuerpo sea
horrible con estas gruesas
sedas, ásperas y espesas,
lo tengo por cosa fea
290 ni mal puesta,
pues es cosa manifiesta
si de oirlo no te enojas,

que estar el árbol sin hojas
es vista muy deshonesta.
Y yo hallo
parecer mal el caballo
si las crines o el cabello
no le cubriesen el cuello,
para mejor adornallo.
300   Por librea
que las cubre y las arrea
tienen las aves la pluma,
y las ovejas en suma
su lana las hermosea.
Y así son
en el cuerpo del varón
la barba y sus aposturas,
y cerdas yertas y duras
para darle perfición.
310   Solamente
tengo en medio de la frente
un ojo: mas aquél es
de un grandísimo pavés,
en grandor no diferente.
Pero ¿qué?
si que el sol mirando de
arriba del alto cielo,
muy bien verá acá en el suelo
cuanto hay y cuanto fue,
320   do llegó;
que no se le encubre, no,
lo que va ni lo que viene;
y si lo miras, no tiene
más de un ojo, como yo.
Pues andar,
a esto debes juntar
que mi padre, el dios Neptuno
como señor solo uno,

reina en ese vuestro mar
330 extendido.
Si me tomas por marido,
con el cual nombre me alegro,
a éste te doy por suegro,
y solamente te pido
que de mí
hayas merced, que me di,
y oyas sin más baldones
mis humildes peticiones,
pues me inclino a sola ti
340 por amor.
Y siendo tan sin pavor,
que al dios Júpiter provoco
y a sus cielos tengo en poco,
y al rayo penetrador,
con desmayo
a ti, ninfa, adoro y trayo
en más estima que a él;
tu saña es más cruel
que ningún golpe de rayo
350 ni furor.
Y aunque siento el disfavor
de verme así desdeñado,
sufriría más pagado
este tu gran desamor
si tú fueses
tan esquiva, que huyeses
a todos como a mí te huyes,
y a los tristes que destruyes
por un rasero midieses.
360 Mas ¿por qué,
dímelo, que no lo sé,
el Cíclope desechado,
a Acis amas de grado
y en tus brazos,

no le pones embarazos,
y en mi despecho le quieres?
O ¿por qué razón prefieres
sus besos a mis abrazos?
370 Mas consiento
que él viva de sí contento,
y a ti, lo que no querría,
para más afrenta mía,
dé también contentamiento,
pues le tiene;
pero si a mis manos viene,
él sentirá que hay en ellas
las fuerzas y las querellas
que a tan gran cuerpo conviene.
380 Con mil sañas
le arrancaré las entrañas
vivas, rompiendo sus pechos.
Y los sus miembros deshechos
sembraré por las campañas
sin abrigo,
como mortal enemigo;
y por esas mesmas ondas
do moras, bravas y hondas,
si se mezclare contigo;
390 porque vivo
me quemo, y el fuego esquivo
que me abrasa y atormenta
más hierve y más se acrecienta
con la injuria que recibo.
Y a mi ver,
tan grave de padecer
es el fuego que me inflama
y la pasión que me llama,
que me parece traer
400 encerrado
el Etna, monte pesado,

con sus fuerzas muy crecidas
y sus llamas encendidas
en mi pecho trasladado.
Tu beldad
no promete crüeldad,
mas ni por ésas un hora
tú, Galatea, señora,
te mueves a piedad.

JUAN BOSCÁN
(1474?–1542)

JUAN BOSCÁN DE ALMOGÁVER was born in Barcelona. He was familiar with the court of Ferdinand of Aragon and was for a time tutor to the Duque de Alba. Later, he became a close friend of Diego Hurtado de Mendoza, Garcilaso de la Vega and Andrea Navagiero, the Venetian ambassador to Spain, at whose suggestion he began to experiment with Italian metres and verse-forms. The meeting with Navagiero took place in 1525; after this, Boscán abandoned *cancionero* poetry and, encouraged by Garcilaso, set out to assimilate Italian models: *terza rima, ottava rima,* the *canzone* and the sonnet. His translation of Castiglione's *Il cortegiano* (1534) is a landmark in the development of Castilian prose. The chief influences on Boscán's later verse are Petrarch and the fifteenth-century Valencian poet Ausias March, a combination which appears in other Castilian poets before 1550. He is an interesting, though uneven, poet, important as an innovator, but overshadowed by the mature achievement of Garcilaso. Many of his poems are flawed by clichés and faulty rhythms; nevertheless, at his best, he conveys his private fears in subtle and memorable images which occasionally anticipate Quevedo. (Both poets have a sonnet which begins: "Cargado voy de mí . . .") Of the poems I have chosen, the first belongs to the early *cancionero* period. The last two are based on passages from Ausias March, and show clearly how Boscán's verse springs to life under the influence of the earlier poet. *Obras poéticas,* ed. M. de Riquer, A. Comas and J. Molas, vol. I, Barcelona, 1957.

22

A SU AMIGA, ENVIÁNDOLE UN CANCIONERO DE SUS COPLAS

Ahí van las ansias mías,
presentes y las pasadas,
do más vivas que pintadas,
hallaréis mis fantasías,
de mi mano trasladadas.
Aunque a otras se presenta
parte aquí de mis querellas,
al rematar de la cuenta,
la suma de todas ellas
10   a vuestra merced se asienta.
Si antes de yo seguiros
lo que hice fue acertado,
de ser ya predestinado
a la gloria de serviros,
parece que fui salvado.
Y si en otras hermosuras
anduvo mi sentimiento,
los males de aquel tormento
no fueron sino figuras
20   deste nuevo pensamiento.

23

Antigua llaga que en mis huesos cría
no deja resollar el buen deseo.
Yo por caminos ásperos rodeo,
por llegar a sosiego el alma mía.
Hurto algún gusto, mas mi fantasía
me le embaraza cuando le poseo.
Medrar no puede aquello que granjeo,
que en tierra se sembró cruda y sombría.

El bien que el seso ofrece al sentimiento,
10   hace que amor me ponga diligencia,
para cerrar mis ojos al tormento.
   Porque bien sé que un blando pensamiento
da causa de tener menos paciencia,
y a veces es peligro estar contento.

24

Dulce soñar y dulce congojarme,
cuando estaba soñando que soñaba.
Dulce gozar con lo que me engañaba,
si un poco más durara el engañarme.
   Dulce no estar en mí que figurarme
podía cuanto bien yo deseaba.
Dulce placer, aunque me importunaba,
que alguna vez llegaba a despertarme.
   ¡O sueño, cuánto más leve y sabroso
10   me fueras, si vinieras tan pesado,
que asentaras en mí con más reposo!
   Durmiendo, en fin, fui bienaventurado,
y es justo en la mentira ser dichoso
quien siempre en la verdad fue desdichado.

25

¡O gran fuerza de amor, que así enflaqueces
los que nacidos son para ser fuertes,
y les truecas así todas sus suertes,
que presto los más ricos empobreces!
   ¡O piélago de mar, que te enriqueces
con los despojos de infinitas muertes!
Trágaslos, y después luego los viertes,
porque nunca en un punto permaneces.
   ¡O rayo, cuyo efeto no entendemos,
10   que de dentro nos dejas abrasados
y de fuera sin mal sanos nos vemos!

¡O dolencia mortal, cuyos extremos
son menos conocidos y alcanzados
por los tristes que más los padecemos!

26

Como aquel que en soñar gusto recibe,
su gusto procediendo de locura,
así el imaginar, con su figura,
vanamente su gozo en mí concibe.
Otro bien, en mí, triste, no se escribe,
sino es aquel que mi pensar procura:
de cuanto ha sido hecho en mi ventura,
lo solo imaginado es lo que vive.
Teme mi corazón de ir adelante,
10 viendo estar su dolor puesto en celada,
y así revuelve atrás en un instante
a contemplar su gloria ya pasada.
¡O sombra de remedio inconstante!:
ser en mí lo mejor lo que no es nada.

27

Como el patrón que, en golfo navegando,
lleva su nao, y viendo claro el cielo,
está más lejos de tener recelo
que si estuviese en tierra paseando:
así yo por lo hondo travesando
de mi querer, que nunca tuvo suelo,
el rato que me hallo estar sin duelo,
que voy seguro luego estoy pensando.
Pero después si el viento mueve guerra
10 y la braveza de la mar levanta,
acude 'l nunca más entrar en barca,
y el voto de ir a ver la casa santa,
y el desear ser labrador en tierra,
mucho más que en la mar un gran monarca.

FRANCISCO SÁ DE MIRANDA
(1481–1558)

Francisco Sá de Miranda was born in Coimbra and studied law at the University of Lisbon. In 1520 he went to Italy, where he came to know a number of Italian writers, including Bembo, Sannazzaro and Ariosto, and was the protégé of Vittoria Colonna, the benefactress of Michelangelo and a distant relative of the Sá family. On his return to Portugal, probably in 1526, he visited the Castilian court, where he met Garcilaso de la Vega and Boscán. Sá de Miranda was the first Portuguese poet to write in the Italianate manner, though he never completely abandoned older models. The sombre, intellectual quality of some of his poetry, as well as its frequent rhythmical lapses, remind one of Boscán. His Castilian poems include numerous sonnets and eclogues and also one of the earliest mythological fables, the *Fábula del Mondego*; nevertheless, in spite of some fine passages, these are generally inferior to his *villancicos*, of which I print two examples. *Obras completas*, ed. M. Rodrigues Lapa, 2 vols., Lisbon, 1942.

28

¡Quién viese aquel día
cuando, cuando, cuando,
saliese mi vida
ya de tanto bando!
　¡Ay, mis tristes ojos,
tan tristes, tan tristes,
vistes mil enojos,
un placer no vistes;
vistes añadida

10   a mi pena pena
     y en tan luenga vida
     nunca una hora buena!
     ¡Si a la suerte mía
     pluguiese, ay, pluguiese
     que viese ora el día
     en que más no viese!

29

     ¡Sola me dejaste
     en aquel yermo!
     ¡Villano malo, gallego!
     Voyme a do te fuiste,
     voyme no sé adónde.
     El valle responde,
     ¡tú no respondiste!
     Moza, sola y triste,
     yo, llorando, ciego;
10   ¡tú pásaslo en juego!
     Por yermos ajenos
     lloro y grito en vano;
     ¡gallego y villano!
     ¿Qué esperaba yo menos?
     ¡Ojos de agua llenos,
     pecho de tal fuego!
     ¿cuándo habréis sosiego?

GARCILASO DE LA VEGA
(1501?–1536)

Garcilaso de la Vega was born in Toledo. His noble ancestry
included two notable fifteenth-century writers, Fernán Pérez de
Guzmán and the Marqués de Santillana. In 1520 he entered the
service of the Emperor Charles V and served in a number of
military actions as a member of the *Guardia real*. Five years later, he
married Doña Elena de Zúñiga; his deepest feelings, however, were
reserved for the Portuguese lady-in-waiting Doña Isabel Freire,
whose marriage and early death are reflected in the First and Third
Eclogues. Garcilaso's close friendship with Boscán made him
him aware of the possibilities of Italianate verse; from a tentative
beginning as a *cancionero* poet, he progressed within a few years to
the maturity of the First Eclogue (1533–4). In 1532, Garcilaso fell
into temporary disfavour with the Emperor, and was imprisoned
for a time on the "isla del Danubio" described in the Third *Canción*.
On his release, he entered the service of the Duque de Alba, Viceroy
of Naples. This was the last decisive step in his poetic career: his
reputation as the greatest Spanish poet of the early Renaissance
rests entirely on the poems written after this date. His stay in
Naples brought him into contact with a number of Italian poets, in-
cluding Luigi Tansillo (1510–1568) and Bernardo Tasso (1493–1569),
from whom he derived the *lira* form used for the first time in the
Fifth *Canción*, and imitated by many later Spanish poets. In 1535,
Garcilaso took part in the Spanish expedition to Tunis, where he
was seriously wounded. The First Elegy, his finest poem apart
from the Eclogues, was written on the death of Bernardino de
Toledo, the brother of the Duque de Alba, who was mortally
wounded in the same action. On 19th September 1536, Garcilaso
met his own death in an ambush near Fréjus while campaigning

in the south of France. His poems were first published in 1543 by Boscán's widow, in a volume entitled *Las obras de Boscán y algunas de Garcilaso*. The later editions and commentaries of Francisco Sánchez de las Brozas (1574), Herrera (1580) and Tamayo de Vargas (1622) already grant him the status of a classic.

With Garcilaso, Spanish Renaissance poetry achieves maturity in the space of a few years. The strength and sensitivity of his best work conceal a remarkable skill in assimilating the themes and techniques of other poets, from Virgil to his Italian contemporaries. In his three Eclogues, the pastoral convention becomes a serious instrument for handling basic human situations; the characteristic melancholy of these poems comes from a Stoic acceptance of experience, deepened by a knowledge of Renaissance ideals of conduct. Between the First and Third Eclogues (the Second is the earliest in order of writing) there is a progressive attempt to overcome the sense of loss symbolized by the death of Isabel Freire, through direct exhortation (in the elegy on Don Bernardino de Toledo), and through the fusion of pastoral and myth in the Third Eclogue. Technical mastery apart, this process is probably the key to Garcilaso's most sustained achievement. I should have liked to include all three poems; failing that, the Third Eclogue must stand as his final and most original statement on the relations between art and experience. *Poesías castellanas completas*, ed. E. L. Rivers, *Clásicos Castalia*, vol. 6, Madrid, 1969.

30

Escrito está en mi alma vuestro gesto,
y cuanto yo escribir de vos deseo;
vos sola lo escribistes, yo lo leo
tan solo, que aun de vos me guardo en esto.

En esto estoy y estaré siempre puesto;
que aunque no cabe en mí cuanto en vos veo,
de tanto bien lo que no entiendo creo,
tomando ya la fe por presupuesto.

Yo no nací sino para quereros:

10 mi alma os ha cortado a su medida;
por hábito del alma misma os quiero.
    Cuanto tengo confieso yo deberos;
por vos nací, por vos tengo la vida,
por vos he de morir y por vos muero.

31

    A Dafne ya los brazos le crecían,
y en luengos ramos vueltos se mostraban;
en verdes hojas vi que se tornaban
los cabellos que al oro escurecían.
    De áspera corteza se cubrían
los tiernos miembros, que aún bullendo estaban;
los blancos pies en tierra se hincaban,
y en torcidas raíces se volvían.
    Aquel que fue la causa de tal daño,
10 a fuerza de llorar, crecer hacía
el árbol que con lágrimas regaba.
    ¡Oh miserable estado, oh mal tamaño!
¡Que con lloralla crezca cada día
la causa y la razón por que lloraba!

32

    En tanto que de rosa y azucena
se muestra la color en vuestro gesto,
y que vuestro mirar ardiente, honesto,
enciende al corazón y lo refrena;
    y en tanto que el cabello, que en la vena
del oro se escogió, con vuelo presto,
por el hermoso cuello blanco, enhiesto,
el viento mueve, esparce y desordena;
    coged de vuestra alegre primavera
10 el dulce fruto, antes que el tiempo airado
cubra de nieve la hermosa cumbre.

Marchitará la rosa el viento helado,
todo lo mudará la edad ligera,
por no hacer mudanza en su costumbre.

33

CANCIÓN TERCERA

Con un manso rüido
de agua corriente y clara,
cerca el Danubio una isla, que pudiera
ser lugar escogido
para que descansara
quien como yo estó agora, no estuviera;
do siempre primavera
parece en la verdura
sembrada de las flores;
10   hacen los ruiseñores
renovar el placer o la tristura
con sus blandas querellas,
que nunca día ni noche cesan dellas.

   Aquí estuve yo puesto,
o por mejor decillo,
preso y forzado y solo en tierra ajena;
bien pueden hacer esto
en quien puede sufrillo
y en quien él a sí mismo se condena.
20   Tengo sólo una pena,
si muero desterrado
y en tanta desventura,
que piensen por ventura
que juntos tantos males me han llevado;
y sé yo bien que muero
por sólo aquello que morir espero.

   El cuerpo está en poder
y en manos de quien puede
hacer a su placer lo que quisiere;

30 mas no podrá hacer
que mal librado quede,
mientras de mí otra prenda no tuviere.
Cuando el mal viniere,
y la postrera suerte,
aquí me ha de hallar,
en el mismo lugar,
que otra cosa más dura que la muerte
me halla y ha hallado;
y esto sabe muy bien quien lo ha probado.
40   No es necesario agora
hablar más sin provecho,
que es mi necesidad muy apretada;
pues ha sido en un hora
todo aquello deshecho
en que toda mi vida fue gastada.
¿Y al fin de tal jornada
presumen espantarme?
Sepan que ya no puedo
morir sino sin miedo;
50 que aun nunca qué temer quiso dejarme
la desventura mía,
que el bien y el miedo me quitó en un día.
    Danubio, río divino,
que por fieras naciones
vas con tus claras ondas discurriendo,
pues no hay otro camino
por donde mis razones
vayan fuera de aquí, sino corriendo
por tus aguas y siendo
60 en ellas anegadas;
si en tierra tan ajena
en la desierta arena
fueren de alguno acaso en fin halladas,
entiérrelas, siquiera,
porque su error se acabe en tu ribera.

Aunque en el agua mueras,
canción, no has de quejarte;
que yo he mirado bien lo que te toca.
Menos vida tuvieras
70 si hubieras de igualarte
con otras que se me han muerto en la boca.
Quién tiene culpa desto,
allá lo entenderás de mí muy presto.

34

ÉGLOGA TERCERA

Aquella voluntad honesta y pura,
ilustre y hermosísima María,
que en mí de celebrar tu hermosura,
tu ingenio y tu valor estar solía,
a despecho y a pesar de la ventura
que por otro camino me desvía,
está y estará en mí tanto clavada,
cuanto del cuerpo el alma acompañada.

Y aun no se me figura que me toca
10 aqueste oficio solamente en vida;
mas con la lengua muerta y fría en la boca
pienso mover la voz a ti debida.
Libre mi alma de su estrecha roca,
por el Estigio lago conducida,
celebrándote irá, y aquel sonido
hará parar las aguas del olvido.

Mas la fortuna, de mi mal no harta,
me aflige y de un trabajo en otro lleva;
ya de la patria, ya del bien me aparta,
20 ya mi paciencia en mil maneras prueba;
y lo que siento más, es que la carta,
donde mi pluma en tu alabanza mueva,
poniendo en su lugar cuidados vanos,
me quita y me arrebata de las manos.

Pero, por más que en mí su fuerza pruebe,
no tornará mi corazón mudable;
nunca dirán jamás que me remueve
fortuna de un estudio tan loable. ·
Apolo y las hermanas, todas nueve,
30   me darán ocio y lengua con que hable
lo menos de lo que en tu ser cupiere,
que esto será lo más que yo pudiere.
    En tanto no te ofenda ni te harte
tratar del campo y soledad que amaste,
ni desdeñes aquesta inculta parte
de mi estilo, que en algo ya estimaste.
Entre las armas del sangriento Marte,
do apenas hay quien su furor contraste,
hurté del tiempo aquesta breve suma,
40   tomando, ora la espada, ora la pluma.
    Aplica, pues, un rato los sentidos
al bajo son de mi zampoña ruda,
indigna de llegar a tus oídos,
pues de ornamento y gracia va desnuda;
mas a las veces son mejor oídos
el puro ingenio y lengua casi muda,
testigos limpios de ánimo inocente,
que la curiosidad del elocuente.
    Por aquesta razón de ti escuchado,
50   aunque me falten otras, ser merezco.
Lo que puedo te doy, y lo que he dado,
con recibillo tú yo me enriquezco.
De cuatro ninfas que del Tajo amado
salieron juntas, a cantar me ofrezco,
Filódoce, Dinámene y Climene,
Nise, que en hermosura par no tiene.
    Cerca del Tajo en soledad amena,
de verdes sauces hay una espesura,
toda de hiedra revestida y llena,
60   que por el tronco va hasta el altura,

y así la teje arriba y encadena,
que el sol no halla paso a la verdura;
el agua baña el prado con sonido
alegrando la vista y el oído.
Con tanta mansedumbre el cristalino
Tajo en aquella parte caminaba,
que pudieran los ojos el camino
determinar apenas que llevaba.
Peinando sus cabellos de oro fino,
70 una ninfa, del agua do moraba,
la cabeza sacó, y el prado ameno
vido de flores y de sombra lleno.
Movióla el sitio umbroso, el manso viento,
el suave olor de aquel florido suelo.
Las aves en el fresco apartamiento
vio descansar del trabajoso vuelo.
Secaba entonces el terreno aliento
el sol subido en la mitad del cielo.
En el silencio sólo se escuchaba
80 un susurro de abejas que sonaba.
Habiendo contemplado una gran pieza
atentamente aquel lugar sombrío,
somorgujó de nuevo su cabeza,
y al fondo se dejó calar del río.
A sus hermanas a contar empieza
del verde sitio el agradable frío,
y que vayan les ruega y amonesta
allí con su labor a estar la siesta.
No perdió en esto mucho tiempo el ruego,
90 que las tres dellas su labor tomaron,
y en mirando de fuera, vieron luego
el prado, hacia el cual enderezaron.
El agua clara con lascivo juego
nadando dividieron y cortaron,
hasta que el blanco pie tocó mojado,
saliendo de la arena, el verde prado.

Poniendo ya en lo enjuto las pisadas,
escurrieron del agua sus cabellos,
los cuales esparciendo, cubijadas
100 las hermosas espaldas fueron dellos.
Luego sacando telas delicadas,
que en delgadeza competían con ellos,
en lo más escondido se metieron,
y a su labor atentas se pusieron.

Las telas eran hechas y tejidas
del oro que el felice Tajo envía,
apurado, después de bien cernidas
las menudas arenas do se cría.

Y de las verdes hojas, reducidas
110 en estambre sutil, cual convenía
para seguir el delicado estilo
del oro ya tirado en rico hilo.

La delicada estambre era distinta
de las colores que antes le habían dado
con la fineza de la varia tinta
que se halla en las conchas del pescado.
Tanto artificio muestra en lo que pinta
y teje cada ninfa en su labrado,
cuanto mostraron en sus tablas antes
120 el celebrado Apeles y Timantes.

Filódoce, que así de aquéllas era
llamada la mayor, con diestra mano
tenía figurada la ribera
de Éstrimón, de una parte el verde llano,
y de otra el monte de aspereza fiera,
pisado tarde o nunca de pie humano,
donde el amor movió con tanta gracia
la dolorosa lengua del de Tracia.

Estaba figurada la hermosa
130 Eurídice, en el blanco pie mordida
de la pequeña sierpe ponzoñosa,
entre la hierba y flores escondida;

descolorida estaba como rosa
que ha sido fuera de sazón cogida,
y el ánima, los ojos ya volviendo,
de su hermosa carne despidiendo.
    Figurado se vía extensamente
el osado marido que bajaba
al triste reino de la escura gente,
140 y la mujer perdida recobraba;
y cómo después desto él, impaciente,
por miralla de nuevo, la tornaba
a perder otra vez, y del tirano
se queja al monte solitario en vano.
    Dinámene no menos artificio
mostraba en la labor que había tejido,
pintando a Apolo en el robusto oficio
de la silvestre caza embebecido.
Mudar luego le hace el ejercicio
150 la vengativa mano de Cupido,
que hizo a Apolo consumirse en lloro
después que le enclavó con punta de oro.
    Dafne, con el cabello suelto al viento,
sin perdonar al blanco pie, corría
por áspero camino tan sin tiento,
que Apolo en la pintura parecía
que, porque ella templase el movimiento,
con menos ligereza la seguía.
Él va siguiendo, y ella huye como
160 quien siente al pecho el odïoso plomo.
    Mas a la fin los brazos le crecían,
y en sendos ramos vueltos se mostraban,
y los cabellos, que vencer solían
al oro fino, en hojas se tornaban;
en torcidas raíces se extendían
los blancos pies, y en tierra se hincaban.
Llora el amante, y busca el ser primero,
besando y abrazando aquel madero.

Climene, llena de destreza y maña,
170 el oro y las colores matizando,
iba de hayas una gran montaña
de robles y de peñas varïando.
Un puerco entre ellas, de braveza extraña,
estaba los colmillos aguzando
contra un mozo, no menos animoso,
con su venablo en mano, que hermoso.

Tras esto, el puerco allí se vía herido,
de aquel mancebo por su mal valiente,
y el mozo en tierra estaba ya tendido,
180 abierto el pecho del rabioso diente;
con el cabello de oro desparcido
barriendo el suelo miserablemente,
las rosas blancas por allí sembradas
tornaba con su sangre coloradas.

Adonis éste se mostraba que era,
según se muestra Venus dolorida,
que viendo la herida abierta y fiera,
estaba sobre él casi amortecida.
Boca con boca coge la postrera
190 parte del aire que solía dar vida
al cuerpo, por quien ella en este suelo
aborrecido tuvo al alto cielo.

La blanca Nise no tomó a destajo
de los pasados casos la memoria,
y en la labor de su sutil trabajo
no quiso entretejer antigua historia;
antes mostrando de su claro Tajo
en su labor la celebrada gloria,
lo figuró en la parte donde él baña
200 la más felice tierra de la España.

Pintado el caudaloso río se vía,
que, en áspera estrecheza reducido,
un monte casi al rededor tenía,
con ímpetu corriendo y con rüido;

querer cercallo todo parecía
en su volver, mas era afán perdido;
dejábase correr, en fin, derecho,
contento de lo mucho que había hecho.
    Estaba puesta en la sublime cumbre
210 del monte, y desde allí por él sembrada,
aquella ilustre y clara pesadumbre,
de antiguos edificios adornada.
De allí con agradable mansedumbre
el Tajo va siguiendo su jornada,
y regando los campos y arboledas
con artificio de las altas ruedas.
    En la hermosa tela se veían
entretejidas las silvestres diosas
salir de la espesura, y que venían
220 todas a la ribera presurosas,
en el semblante tristes, y traían
cestillos blancos de purpúreas rosas,
las cuales esparciendo, derramaban
sobre una ninfa muerta que lloraban.
    Todas con el cabello desparcido
lloraban una ninfa delicada,
cuya vida mostraba que había sido
antes de tiempo y casi en flor cortada.
Cerca del agua, en un lugar florido,
230 estaba entre la hierba degollada,
cual queda el blanco cisne cuando pierde
la dulce vida entre la hierba verde.
    Una de aquellas diosas, que en belleza,
al parecer, a todas excedía,
mostrando en el semblante la tristeza
que del funesto y triste caso había,
apartada algún tanto, en la corteza
de un álamo unas letras escribía,
como epitafio de la ninfa bella,
240 que hablaban así por parte della:

"Elisa soy, en cuyo nombre suena
y se lamenta el monte cavernoso,
testigo del dolor y grave pena
en que por mí se aflige Nemoroso,
y llama Elisa; Elisa a boca llena
responde el Tajo, y lleva presuroso
al mar Lusitania el nombre mío,
donde será escuchado, yo lo fío."

En fin, en esta tela artificiosa
250   toda la historia estaba figurada,
que en aquella ribera deleitosa
de Nemoroso fue tan celebrada;
porque de todo aquesto y cada cosa
estaba Nise ya tan informada,
que llorando el pastor, mil veces ella
se enterneció escuchando su querella.

Y porque aqueste lamentable cuento,
no sólo entre las selvas se contase,
mas, dentro de las ondas, sentimiento
260   con la noticia desto se mostrase,
quiso que de su tela el argumento
la bella ninfa muerta señalase,
y así se publicase de uno en uno
por el húmido reino de Neptuno.

Destas historias tales varïadas
eran las telas de las cuatro hermanas,
las cuales, con colores matizadas,
claras las luces, de las sombras vanas
mostraban a los ojos relevadas
270   las cosas y figuras que eran llanas;
tanto que, al parecer, el cuerpo vano
pudiera ser tomado con la mano.

Los rayos ya del sol se trastornaban,
escondiendo su luz, al mundo cara,
tras altos montes, y a la luna daban
lugar para mostrar su blanca cara;

los peces a menudo ya saltaban,
con la cola azotando el agua clara,
cuando las ninfas, la labor dejando,
280   hacia el agua se fueron paseando.

En las templadas ondas ya metidos
tenían los pies, y reclinar querían
los blancos cuerpos, cuando sus oídos
fueron de dos zampoñas que tañían
suave y dulcemente, detenidos;
tanto, que sin mudarse las oían
y al son de las zampoñas escuchaban
dos pastores, a veces, que cantaban.

Más claro cada vez el son se oía,
290   de dos pastores, que venían cantando
tras el ganado, que también venía
por aquel verde soto caminando,
y a la majada, ya pasado el día,
recogido llevaban, alegrando
las verdes selvas con el son süave,
haciendo su trabajo menos grave.

Tirreno destos dos el uno era,
Alcino el otro, entrambos estimados,
y sobre cuantos pacen la ribera
300   del Tajo, con sus vacas, enseñados;
mancebos de una edad, de una manera
a cantar juntamente aparejados,
y a responder, aquesto van diciendo,
cantando el uno, el otro respondiendo.

TIRRENO

Flérida, para mí dulce y sabrosa
más que la fruta del cercado ajeno,
más blanca que la leche y más hermosa
que el prado por abril, de flores lleno;
si tú respondes pura y amorosa

310   al verdadero amor de tu Tirreno,
a mi majada arribarás, primero
que el cielo nos amuestre su lucero.

ALCINO

Hermosa Filis, siempre yo te sea
amargo al gusto más que la retama,
y de ti despojado yo me vea,
cual queda el tronco de su verde rama,
si más que yo el murciélago desea
la escuridad, ni más la luz desama,
por ver ya el fin de un término tamaño
320   deste día, para mí mayor que un año.

TIRRENO

Cual suele acompañada de su bando
aparecer la dulce primavera,
cuando Favonio y Céfiro soplando,
al campo tornan su beldad primera,
y van artificiosos esmaltando
de rojo, azul y blanco la ribera,
en tal manera a mí, Flérida mía,
viniendo, reverdece mi alegría.

ALCINO

¿Ves el furor del animoso viento,
330   embravecido en la fragosa sierra,
que los antiguos robles ciento a ciento
y los pinos altísimos atierra,
y de tanto destrozo aún no contento,
al espantoso mar mueve la guerra?
Pequeña es esta furia, comparada
a la de Filis, con Alcino airada.

TIRRENO

El blanco trigo multiplica y crece,
produce el campo en abundancia tierno
pasto al ganado, el verde monte ofrece
340 a las fieras salvajes su gobierno;
a doquiera que miro me parece
que derrama la copia todo el cuerno;
mas todo se convertirá en abrojos
si dello aparta Flérida sus ojos.

ALCINO

De la esterilidad es oprimido
el monte, el campo, el soto y el ganado;
la malicia del aire corrompido
hace morir la hierba mal su grado;
las aves ven su descubierto nido,
350 que ya de verdes hojas fue cercado;
pero si Filis por aquí tornare,
hará reverdecer cuanto mirare.

TIRRENO

El álamo de Alcides escogido
fue siempre, y el laurel del rojo Apolo;
de la hermosa Venus fué tenido
en precio y en estima el mirto solo;
el verde sauz de Flérida es querido,
y por suyo entre todos escogiólo;
doquiera que de hoy más sauces se hallen,
360 el álamo, el laurel y el mirto callen.

ALCINO

El fresno por la selva en hermosura
sabemos ya que sobre todos vaya,
y en aspereza y monte de espesura

se aventaja la verde y alta haya,
mas el que la beldad de tu figura
dondequiera mirado, Filis, haya,
al fresno y a la haya en su aspereza
confesará que vence tu belleza.—

    Esto cantó Tirreno, y esto Alcino
370 le respondió; y habiendo ya acabado
el dulce son, siguieron su camino
con paso un poco más apresurado.
Siendo a las ninfas ya el rumor vecino,
todas juntas se arrojan por el vado,
y de la blanca espuma que movieron
las cristalinas ondas se cubrieron.

DIEGO HURTADO DE MENDOZA
(1503–1575)

Diego Hurtado de Mendoza was born in Granada. The high status of the Mendoza family led him to a series of important diplomatic posts; he was ambassador in London, Venice and Rome and later governor of Siena. In 1568, as the result of a quarrel with Don Diego de Leiva, he was banished to Granada, though he was allowed to return to Madrid in the last year of his life. Hurtado de Mendoza was a friend and contemporary of Boscán and Garcilaso; his political standing undoubtedly helped to establish the new Italianate poetry. His gifts as a humanist—he was a notable linguist and a bibliophile—appear in his remarkable historical work, *La guerra de Granada*, published posthumously in 1627. Several of his poems in older metres are very fine, and his satires and verse-epistles, especially the *Epístola a Boscán*, show an attractive, if at times mordant, sense of humour. His Italianate poems owe a good deal to Petrarch and Tansillo; their technique is often inferior to the quality of their content, though the two sonnets I have included are among the exceptions. *Obras poéticas*, ed. W. Knapp, Madrid, 1877.

35

REDONDILLAS

Va y viene mi pensamiento
como el mar seguro y manso;
¿cuándo tendrá algún descanso
tan continuo movimiento?

GLOSA

Parte el pensamiento mío
cargado de mil dolores,
y vuélveme con mayores
de la parte do le envío.
   Aunque desto en la memoria
10 se engendra tanto contento,
que con tan dulce tormento,
cargado de pena y gloria,
va y viene mi pensamiento.
   Como el mar muy sosegado
se regala con la calma,
así se regala el alma
con tan dichoso cuidado.
   Mas allí mudanza alguna
no puede haber, pues descanso
20 con el mal que me importuna,
que no es sujeto a fortuna,
como el mar seguro y manso.
   Si el cielo se muestra airado,
la mar luego se embravece,
y mientras el mar más crece,
está más firme en su estado.
   Ni a mí me cansa el penar,
ni yo con el mal me canso;
si algo me podrá cansar,
30 es venir a imaginar
cuándo tendrá algún descanso.
   Que aunque en el más firme amor
mil mudanzas puede haber,
como es de pena a placer
y de descanso a dolor,
    sólo en mí está reservado

en tan fijo y firme asiento;
que sin poder ser mudado,
está quedo y sosegado
40 tan continuo movimiento.

36

Nadie fíe en alegría,
porque ninguna hay tan cierta,
a quien no cierre algún día
fortuna o amor la puerta.
Yo vi leche reposada
tornar cortada y aceda,
y vi voluntad trocada
cuando pudiera estar queda.
Yo vi la mar en bonanza
10 levantarse hasta el cielo,
y vi firme confianza
derribada por el suelo.
Amistad hay que se muestra
sola y clara y sin ofensa,
y cuando pensáis que es vuestra
halláisla turbia y suspensa.
Tal os tiene hoy por amigo,
que mañana, si le place,
os tomará por testigo
20 de los agravios que os hace.
Dulce y vano atrevimiento,
poner confianza alguna
sobre tan flaco cimiento
como esperanza y fortuna.
Adonde un bien se concierta
hay un mal que lo desvía;
mas el bien viene y no acierta,
y el mal acierta y porfía.

37

A UN RETRATO

Tu gracia, tu valor, tu hermosura,
muestra de todo el cielo retratada,
como cosa que está sobre natura,
ni pudiera ser vista ni pintada.
Pero ya que en el alma tu figura
tengo, en humana forma abrevïada,
tal hice retraerte de pintura,
cual amor te dejó en ella estampada.
No por ambición vana o por memoria
10 de ti, ni para publicar mis males,
no por verte más veces que te veo;
mas por sólo gozar de tanta gloria,
señora, con los ojos corporales,
como con los del alma y del deseo.

38

Cual simple mariposa vuelvo al fuego
de vuestra hermosura do me abraso,
y cuando siento el daño y huyo el paso
Amor me torna allí por fuerza luego.
No bastan a aliviarme fuerza o ruego,
y si que alguna vez me escapo acaso,
hallo que Amor me está aguardando el paso,
y tórname cual fugitivo al fuego.
Y viendo ya que con vivir no puedo
10 huir de mi destino y fiero suerte,
deseoso en tanto mal de algún sosiego,
perdido a mi tormento todo el miedo,
buscando como Fénix vida en muerte,
cual simple mariposa vuelvo al fuego.

SEBASTIÁN DE HOROZCO
(1510?–1580)

Sebastián de Horozco was born in Toledo, whose history is described in his prose *Relaciones*. He was the father of Sebastián de Covarrubias, the compiler of the famous *Tesoro de la lengua castellana* (1611). His *Cancionero* contains some excellent *glosas a lo divino*, and shows an instinctive skill in the re-creation of popular songs. *Cancionero*, ed. Bibliófilos andaluces, Seville, 1874.

39

SOBRE LA CANCIÓN VIEJA Y MAL ENTENDIDA,
QUE DICE ASÍ:

> Señor Gómez Arias,
> doleos de mí,
> soy mochacha y niña
> y nunca en tal me vi.
>
> Señor Gómez Arias,
> vos me trajistes,
> y en tierra de moros
> vos me vendistes.
> Yo no sé la causa
> 10 porque lo hecistes,
> que yo sin ventura
> no os lo merecí.
>   Señor Gómez Arias, etc.
>
> Si mi triste madre
> tal cosa supiese,
> con sus mesmas manos

la muerte se diese.
No hay hombre en el mundo
que no se doliese
20   de la desventura
que vino por mí.
    Señor Gómez Arias, etc.

En cas de mi padre
estaba encerrada,
de chicos y grandes
querida y mirada.
Véome ora triste
e enajenada,
triste fue la hora
30   en que yo nací.
    Señor Gómez Arias, etc.

Señor Gómez Arias,
habed compasión
de la sin ventura
que queda en prisión.
Conmueva mi llanto
vuestro corazón;
no seáis tan cruel
en dejarme así.
40   Señor Gómez Arias, etc.

Señor Gómez Arias,
si a Córdoba fuerdes,
a mi padre y madre
me encomendedes;
y de mis hermanos
vos os guardedes,
que no os den la muerte
por amor de mí.
    Señor Gómez Arias, etc.

SANTA TERESA DE JESÚS
(1515–1582)

TERESA DE CEPEDES Y AHUMADA was born in Ávila. In 1534 she entered the Carmelite order, and in 1562 founded the convent of San José de Ávila. Her plans for the reform of her order were carried out in the face of much opposition from the civil and religious authorities. In part of this work she was closely associated with San Juan de La Cruz; with him, she is the greatest of the sixteenth-century Castilian mystics. Most of her writing consists of prose works, of which the finest are *Las moradas* and the *Libro de su vida*, her spiritual autobiography. She was canonized in 1622. Her poetic production is slight, but contains a number of very attractive *villancicos*. One of the two famous glosses on the theme "Vivo sin vivir en mí . . ." (the other is by San Juan de la Cruz) is commonly attributed to her. In the poem I have included, the four-line theme is an *a lo divino* version of a song which appears in the *Cancionero* of Montemayor (1554): "Véante mis ojos / y muérame yo luego, / dulce amor mío, / lo que yo más quiero". *Biblioteca de autores españoles*, vol. 53, Madrid, 1930.

40

Véante mis ojos,
dulce Jesús bueno;
véante mis ojos,
muérame yo luego.

Vea quien quisiere
rosas y jazmines,
que si yo te viere,
veré mil jardines:

flor de serafines,
10 Jesús Nazareno,
véante mis ojos,
muérame yo luego.
   No quiero contento
mi Jesús ausente,
que todo es tormento
a quien esto siente;
sólo me sustente
tu amor y deseo,
véante mis ojos,
20 dulce Jesús bueno;
véante mis ojos,
muérame yo luego.

HERNANDO DE ACUÑA
(1518–1580?)

HERNANDO DE ACUÑA was born in Valladolid, of a noble family. He enlisted in the Imperial army at the age of eighteen, and served in the Piedmont campaign as an infantry captain. In 1544, he was captured by the French at Ceresola; after his release, he took part in further campaigns in central Europe and was entrusted by Charles V with a number of diplomatic missions. In 1560 he returned to Spain and married. Little is known of the last years of his life, though his friendship with Hurtado de Mendoza probably dates from this time. In 1553 he had published a verse translation of the *Chevalier délibéré* of the Burgundian poet Olivier de la Marche, from a prose version possibly written by Charles V himself. His other poems were published posthumously by his widow in 1591. Apart from a mythological poem, the *Fábula de Adonis*, and a partial translation of the *Orlando innamorato* of Boiardo (1441–1494), Acuña runs skilfully, though a little mechanically, through most of the Italian repertoire. His best-known poem, the sonnet *Al Rey nuestro señor*, is an effective piece of political propaganda, inferior in literary quality to his pastoral sonnets, one of which is printed here. The second poem is less vivid, but builds up to a stronger climax. *Varias poesías*, ed. E. Catena de Vidal, Madrid, 1954.

41

Un novillo feroz y un fuerte toro
lidian, delante de su becerra amada,
y mirábalos Silvia descuidada,
de gracia y de beldad rico tesoro.
    Cuando por la ribera un sacro coro

de ninfas vi venir, y en su llegada
fue dellas mi pastora coronada
de flores que eran perlas sobre oro;
   y como el fuerte vencedor furioso
10 dio alegre fin a la obstinada empresa,
zampoña no quedó que no tocase
   diciendo: O bien nacido y venturoso
Silvano, si tu llanto, que no cesa,
con fin tan venturoso se acabase.

42

Como vemos que un río mansamente
por do no halla estorbo, sin sonido,
sigue su natural curso seguido,
tal que aun apenas murmurar se siente;
   pero si topa algún inconveniente
rompe con fuerza y pasa con rüido,
tanto que de muy lejos es sentido
el alto y gran rumor de la corriente:
   por sosegado curso semejante
10 fueron un tiempo mis alegres días,
sin que queja o pasión de mí se oyese;
   mas como se me puso amor delante,
la gran corriente de las ansias mías
fue fuerza que en el mundo se sintiese.

GUTIERRE DE CETINA
(1514/17–1554/57)

GUTIERRE DE CETINA was born in Seville. After a period at court, he accompanied Diego Hurtado de Mendoza on his mission to the First Council of Trent (1542) and later served as a soldier in Italy and Germany. In 1543, he spent some months at the court of Milan, where a number of his early love poems were written. On his return to Spain, he lived for several years in Seville; his friendships with Montemayor and Castillejo probably date from this period. Some time after 1550 he settled in Mexico, where he had family connections, and where he probably died from wounds received in a street brawl in Puebla de los Ángeles. Cetina is the best and most prolific of the early followers of Garcilaso. As a sonnet-writer, he draws on a wider range of simile than any of his contemporaries, though his choice of models is less discriminating. Herrera's judgement is fair and accurate: "en número, lengua, terneza y afectos ninguno le negará lugar entre los primeros; mas fáltale el espíritu y vigor . . . y así, dice muchas cosas dulcemente, pero sin fuerzas". There is no doubt, however, that Cetina enlarges the scope of the Petrarchan sonnet more than any Spanish poet before Herrera. His "Ojos claros, serenos . . .", the most famous madrigal in the language, uses an Italian form to embody what is basically a *cancionero* poem. *Obras*, ed. Hazañas, 2 vols., Seville, 1895.

43

Ojos claros, serenos,
si de un dulce mirar sois alabados,
¿por qué, si me miráis, miráis airados?

69

Si cuanto más piadosos,
más bellos parecéis a aquel que os mira,
no me miréis con ira,
porque no parezcáis menos hermosos.
¡Ay, tormentos rabiosos!
Ojos claros, serenos,
10   ya que así me miráis, miradme al menos.

44

Por vos ardí, señora, y por vos ardo
y arder por vos mientras viviere espero,
o contraste el deseo el hado fiero,
o sea favorable al bien que aguardo.

Tan a lo vivo ha penetrado el dardo
de Amor, que, cuando menos bien os quiero,
morir por vos deseo, y por vos muero,
y por vos sola de morir me guardo.

Vos el primer ardor fuisteis al alma;
10   vos último seréis en la última hora,
y creed a mi fe lo que os promete.

Bien podrá de mí muerte haber la palma,
mas después se verá, cual es ahora,
pasar el fuego mío allá de Lete.

45

Como garza real, alta en el cielo,
entre halcones puesta y rodeada,
que siendo de los unos remontada,
de los otros seguirse deja a vuelo,

viendo su muerte acá bajo en el suelo
por oculta virtud manifestada,
no tan presto será de él aquejada
que a voces mostrará su desconsuelo;

las pasadas locuras, los ardores
10   que por otras sentí, fueron, señora,

para me levantar remontadores;
   pero viéndoos a vos, mi matadora,
el alma dio señal en sus temores
de la muerte que paso cada hora.

46

   Horas alegres que pasáis volando
porque a vueltas del bien mayor mal sienta;
sabrosa noche que en tan dulce afrenta
el triste despedir me vas mostrando;
   importuno reloj que, apresurando
tu curso, mi dolor me representa;
estrellas con quien nunca tuve cuenta,
que mi partida vais acelerando;
   gallo que mi pesar has denunciado,
10 lucero que mi luz va obscureciendo,
y tú, mal sosegada y moza Aurora,
   si en vos cabe dolor de mi cuidado,
id poco a poco el paso deteniendo,
si no puede ser más, siquiera un hora.

GREGORIO SILVESTRE
(1520–1569)

Gregorio Silvestre's birthplace is uncertain, though evidence suggests that he was an *extremeño*. In 1541 he became organist of the Cathedral of Granada, where he knew a number of poets, including Hurtado de Mendoza. He was an accomplished musician; though none of his compositions has survived, it seems certain that many of his religious *villancicos* were written for church performance. Silvestre is a remarkable and unjustly neglected poet: his *glosas a lo divino* and other poems in traditional metres are among the best of their kind, and his long *Elegía a la muerte de Doña María Manrique*, though uneven, contains some of the finest elegiac poetry of the period. The tone of his best sonnets is unmistakable; as Rodríguez Moñino has said: "Gregorio Silvestre erige en norma de vida las inquietudes meramente retóricas, en la mayoría de los casos, de sus coetáneos". Several of his poems, like the second of those printed here, show an effective use of colloquialisms for a serious purpose which looks forward to Góngora and Quevedo. *Poesías*, ed. A. Marín Ocete, Granada, 1939.

47

Decid los que tratáis de agricultura
en este valle umbroso y desabrido:
¿qué fruto del deleite habéis tenido
que no se os torne luego en amargura?
Del gusto y del regalo y la dulzura
¿qué espigas y qué grano habéis cogido
que no salga nublado y revenido
del silo de la triste sepultura?

Del mal terreno y mala sementera
10 ¿qué se puede segar, sino sospecha,
disgusto, confusión, remordimiento?
El alma siente ya desde la era
cómo ha de baratar de la cosecha
agosto seco, de eternal tormento.

48

La vida se nos pasa, el tiempo vuela,
las Parcas van obrando por su estilo,
Atropos muy apriesa corta el hilo,
la Muerte hace mangas desta tela.
Y va ya la cargada navezuela
batida de las ondas deste Nilo,
el aire vital sopla, arde el pabilo,
consúmese el humor, muere la vela.
Pasando del peligro a la tormenta,
10 de la fortuna al mal y al accidente,
perdemos, si es perder, tan triste vida.
Y desta vida tal hacemos cuenta
y olvídase la que es eternamente
de gozo incomparable y sin medida.

49

Mortales: ¿habéis visto mayor cosa
que siendo muerte me he tornado vida
y de áspera, crüel y desabrida
me he hecho blanda, dulce y amorosa?
Ya me codician todos por hermosa,
y de quien era más aborrecida
soy con alegre cara recibida,
por suerte deseada y venturosa.

¿Sabéis de qué manera el mortal velo
10   del alma santa desaté de aquella
por quien era el vivir dulce, agradable?
Murió doña María y subió al cielo;
quedó hecho el vivir muerte sin ella,
y alegre vida, yo, dulce y afable.

JUAN DE TIMONEDA
(d. 1583)

JUAN DE TIMONEDA, one of the most important sixteenth-century Spanish dramatists, was a Valencian. Little is known of his life: he worked first as a tanner, and later as a bookseller and actor. Apart from his *comedias* and *autos sacramentales*, he wrote prose fiction in the manner of Boccaccio and Bandello (*El Patrañuelo*, 1567) and published many poems in *cancioneros* and *pliegos sueltos*. His *Rosa de romances* (1573) is one of the most extensive collections of original ballads of its period. The first of the poems included here is another variation on the theme of *la malmaridada* (see p. 6); the second is a vigorous re-working of the well-known poem by the Marqués de Santillana (1398–1458), *A sus fijas, loando la su fermosura*. *Obras*, ed. E. Juliá, 3 vols., Madrid, 1947–8.

50

Soy garridica
y vivo penada
por ser mal casada.
   Yo soy, no repuno,
hermosa sin cuento,
amada de uno,
querida de ciento.
No tengo contento
no valgo ya nada
10   por ser mal casada.
   Con estos cabellos
de bel parecer
haría con ellos

los hombres perder.
Quien los puede haber
no los tiene en nada
por ser mal casada.

51

Tres serranas he encontrado
al pie de una gran montaña,
que, según su gesto y maña,
no deben guardar ganado.
De seda traían y bellos
los velos y gorguerinas,
cordones de perlas finas
apretando sus cabellos,
rubios eran todos ellos
10   y de seda las servillas,
de escarlata las basquillas,
los monjiles de brocado.
De laurel muy adornadas
traían sus tres guirnaldas,
con diamantes y esmeraldas,
en ejorcas y arracadas;
antiparas plateadas,
de carmesín los zurrones,
de marfil con sus tachones
20   cada una su cayado.
Ruecas de oro en su cintura
traían y prendederos,
de aljófar los rocaderos,
los husos de plata pura,
seda hilando con mesura
y cantando esta canción:
"¿Dónde está mi corazón?"
por un valle se han entrado.

JORGE DE MONTEMAYOR
(1520?–1561)

JORGE DE MONTEMAYOR is best known as the author of the pastoral
novel *La Diana* (1559?). He was Portuguese by birth, though pro-
bably of Jewish ancestry. His career as a professional musician
took him to the Castilian court, where he was *cantor de capilla* to the
Infanta María, sister of Philip II, whom he probably accompanied
on his visit to England in 1554. He later took part in the war in
Flanders, and was killed in a quarrel with a rival lover in Piedmont.
Montemayor was a friend of several poets, including Sá de Miranda
and Cetina, and translated the poems of Ausias March into Cas-
tilian. His original verse was collected in his *Cancionero* (1554) and
Segundo cancionero espiritual (1558). In 1559, his religious poems were
condemned by the Inquisition; the best of them, like the longer of
the two included here, reflect the tradition of evangelical Chris-
tianity which derives from Erasmus and Savonarola. To quote
Marcel Bataillon: "Montemayor fue uno de los primeros que
sintieron la grave música de los Salmos, y el primero, sin duda, que
intentó hacerla cantar en castellano con el ritmo nuevo del
hendecasílabo". The first poem included here belongs to a se-
quence of twenty meditations on the Psalm *Miserere mei, Deus.
Cancionero*, ed. A. González Palencia, Madrid, 1932. This does not
include the *Segundo cancionero espiritual* (Antwerp, 1558), of which no
modern edition exists.

52

CÁNTICA

Cor mundum crea in me, Deus,
et spiritum rectum innova in visceribus meis.
Cría en mí, Señor corazón limpio,
y espíritu derecho renueva en mis entrañas.

En mí cría, Señor, corazón limpio,
pues me desamparó el que yo tenía;
de su salud está muy olvidado,
sin camino se anda y sin provecho.
Salido es de su tierra, y peregrino
se anda en vanidades, como loco;
llaméle, y nunca quiso responderme,
que sus pecados proprios le vendieron.
Pues cría en mí, Señor, corazón nuevo,
10   corazón limpio, manso y muy humilde,
pacífico, benigno y pïadoso,
que al prójimo no haga mal ni diga,
no vuelva mal por mal como solía,
mas cumpla rectamente tu precepto.
Y sobre cuantos hay, ame a ti solo,
de ti piense contino y de ti hable,
y gracias te dé siempre por tus obras,
en los himnos y cantos se deleite.
Y aunque en la tierra esté, allá en el cielo
20   esté, converse y loe tu figura.
Tal corazón como éste cría luego,
hazlo de nada, y presto, pues que puedes.
Y sea el corazón tal por tu gracia,
cual por naturaleza ser no puede.
Que la gracia del alma de ti viene
por creación divina, y luego hace
más claro el corazón que sol ni luna.

Ésta es quien las virtudes trae consigo,
y quien todos los vicios echa fuera.
30   Espíritu derecho en mis entrañas
renueva, y traerme ha por buen camino,
y de toda afección mala y terrena
limpio me dejará, y quedaré libre,
y subirme ha a las cosas celestiales;
juntarme ha por amor con todas ellas,
el proprio me hará que yo las ame,
y el amador y amado por la fuerza
de aquel amor, se hacen ambos uno.
Pues luego aquel espíritu que amare
40   las obras corporales será cuerpo,
y aquel solo espíritu, que ama
las obras del espíritu perfecto.
Pues dame un tal espíritu, que suba
a tu contemplación continamente.
Que espíritu eres tú, Señor eterno,
y espíritu han de ser los que te adoran,
que en espíritu limpio y verdadero
quieres ser adorado justamente.
Pues dame tú espíritu que busque
50   las cosas tuyas proprias, no las suyas,
y no lo que él quisiere, sino aquello
de que tú, gran Señor, fueres servido.
Renueva en mis entrañas, que están muertas,
un espíritu nuevo, y aun de nuevo
en este pecador debes hacelle:
que aquel que tú primero en mí pusiste,
mis males le ahogaron, y mis culpas.
Dame espíritu nuevo que renueve
lo que es por mi pecado envejecido.
60   Mi alma ame a ti naturalmente
como a su Señor proprio, sobre todos.
Que el amor natural es muy derecho,
por cuanto de tu solo amor procede;

pero su voluntad mala e inicua
la tiene en sí el pecado envejecida,
y este amor natural está embotado.
Pues renueva, Señor, con gracia tuya
este amor, porque vuelva en este punto
a su naturaleza, y a ti ame,
70 y a ti solo desee, y a ti quiera,
Y este amor sea tan firme en mis entrañas,
que allí eche raíces y florezca
mi ánima, y dé fruto de alabanzas;
y de tal suerte quede, que peligro
de muerte ni otra cosa no le impida
a estar conforme a ti, que le criaste.

53

¡Sea bienvenido, sea,
sea bienvenido!,
el Verbo hijo del padre,
¡sea bienvenido!
Hoy nació de Virgen madre,
¡sea bienvenido!,
el Verbo del padre hijo,
¡sea bienvenido!
Hoy nació con regocijo.
10 ¡Sea bienvenido!

LUIS DE CAMOENS
(1524–1579)

Luis de Camoens, the great Portuguese writer and author of the verse-epic *Os Lusíadas*, also composed a large number of shorter poems in Portuguese and Castilian. His poems in traditional metres show great feeling for both *cancionero* and popular verse. As a lyric poet in the Italianate manner, Camoens is a talented follower of Garcilaso, whom he translated and imitated. Occasionally, as in the sonnet printed here, he goes beyond earlier Renaissance models to achieve a type of complexity more characteristic of the seventeenth century. *Lírica*, ed. J. M. Rodrigues and A. Lopes Vieira, Coimbra, 1932.

54

REDONDILLAS

De dentro tengo mi mal,
que de fuera no hay señal.
　Mi nueva y dulce querella
es invisible a la gente;
el alma sola la siente,
que el cuerpo no es digno della.
Como la viva centella
se encubre en el pedernal,
de dentro tengo mi mal.

55

Irme quiero, madre,
a aquella galera,
con el marinero
a ser marinera.
   Madre, si me fuere,
do quiera que vo,
no lo quiero yo,
que el Amor lo quiere.
Aquel niño fiero
10 hace que me mueva
por un marinero
a ser marinera.
   Él, que todo puede,
madre, no podrá,
pues el alma va,
que el cuerpo se quede.
Con él, por quien muero
voy, porque no muera;
que si es marinero,
20 seré marinera.
   Es tirana ley
del niño señor,
que por un amor
se deseche un rey.
Pues desta manera
quiero irme, quiero,
por un marinero
a ser marinera.
   Decid, ondas, ¿cuándo
30 vistes vos doncella,
siendo tierna y bella,
andar navegando?

Mas ¿qué no se espera
de aquel niño fiero?
Vea yo quien quiero:
sea marinera.

56

El vaso reluciente y cristalino,
de ángeles agua clara y olorosa,
de blanca seda ornado y fresca rosa,
ligado con cabellos de oro fino,
   bien claro parecía el don divino
labrado por la mano artificiosa
de aquella blanca ninfa, gracïosa
más que el rubio lucero matutino.
   Nel vaso vuestro corpo se afigura,
10 rajado de los blandos miembros bellos,
y en el agua vuestra ánima pura;
   la seda es la blancura, y los cabellos
son las prisiones, y la ligadura
con que mi libertad fue asida dellos.

JERÓNIMO DE LOMAS CANTORAL
(c. 1540–1600)

JERÓNIMO DE LOMAS CANTORAL was born in Valladolid, where he
belonged to a group of poets which at one time included Acuña.
His *Obras* (1578) contain a translation of the *Piscatorias* of Tansillo
and original poems in both the *cancionero* and Italianate manners.
Lomas is a good example of a minor Petrarchan who continues to
use older verse-forms without any sense that they are archaic or
unfashionable. The sonnet which I include shows a skilful and
moving use of night imagery reminiscent of Francisco de la Torre.
Obras, Madrid, 1578. There is no modern edition.

57

Ya de mis quietos días el sereno
cielo se va turbando y, con sosiego,
en el alma se enciende un nuevo fuego
que me consume dulcemente el seno.
   Recoge, corazón, recoge el freno
y a más sano lugar te vuelve luego,
pues que de amor el más sabroso juego
está con hiel templado y con veneno.
   Al sospirar y al llanto triste y laso,
a oscura luz y a noches congojosas
no tornes, ya que miras libre al cielo.
   Huye a los ojos bellos, cierra el paso
al vano desear y a mentirosas
esperanzas, y cércate de hielo.

FRAY LUIS DE LEÓN
(1527–1591)

Luis de León was born in Belmonte (Cuenca). He studied in Madrid and Valladolid, where his father was a court advocate, and later attended three universities: Salamanca, Toledo and Alcalá. He entered the Augustinian order in 1544, and in 1561 was appointed to the first of a number of Chairs at the University of Salamanca. From 1572–6 he was imprisoned by order of the Inquisition for his views concerning the interpretation of the Scriptures and the authority of the Vulgate. After a protracted trial, embittered by the current rivalry between the Augustinian and Dominican orders, he was declared innocent and returned in triumph to Salamanca, where a new Chair of Theology was created for him in 1577. In 1578 he was appointed to the commission for the reform of the Gregorian calendar and entrusted with the editing of the works of Santa Teresa de Jesús. He died in 1591, a few days after being elected Provincial of his order in Castile. Luis de León was an outstanding classical and Hebrew scholar, and an untiring translator and commentator of Biblical texts. His meticulous training as a philologist is reflected in his concept of style: "(el buen hablar es) negocio que de las palabras que todos hablan elige las que convienen y mira el sonido dellas, y aun cuenta a veces las letras, y las pesa y las mide y las compone, para que no solamente digan con claridad lo que se pretende decir, sino también con armonía y dulzura". The finest and most extensive of his Castilian prose works (he was also a copious writer in Latin) is *De los nombres de Cristo* (1583), a meditation in dialogue form on the virtues of Christ, which offers many points of comparison with the poems. His numerous verse translations from Virgil, Horace, Petrarch and other classical and Renaissance poets show great sensitivity and verbal skill. Compared with these, the body of his original poems is small, and confined to only a few major themes. Their typical content is a combination of Christian and Platonic doctrine, shaped in the *lira* form, and intensified by a deep sense of spiritual isolation. No other poet of this century writes with such feeling both of the corruption of worldly values and of the soul's need to find harmony in God; as Dámaso Alonso has said: "Entre armonía y desarmonía se polariza todo el arte de Fray Luis". In his less successful work, the failure to reach a point of balance gives rise to structural flaws and a tendency to diffuseness; the best of his odes, however, have an intricacy of thematic structure and a sweeping melodic quality which raise them to the level of great poetry. Fray Luis's poems were published for the first time by Quevedo in 1631. *The original poems*, ed. E. Sarmiento, Manchester U.P., 1953. *Poesías*, ed. P. Ángel C. Vega O.S.A., Madrid, 1955.

58

VIDA RETIRADA

   ¡Qué descansada vida
la del que huye el mundanal rüido,
y sigue la escondida
senda, por donde han ido
los pocos sabios que en el mundo han sido!
   Que no le enturbia el pecho
de los soberbios grandes el estado,
ni del dorado techo
se admira, fabricado
10   del sabio moro, en jaspes sustentado.
   No cura si la fama
canta con voz su nombre pregonera;
no cura si encarama
la lengua lisonjera

lo que condena la verdad sincera.
   ¿Qué presta a mi contento,
si soy del vano dedo señalado,
si en busca de este viento
ando desalentado
20 con ansias vivas, y mortal cuidado?
   ¡Oh, campo! ¡Oh, monte! ¡Oh, río!
¡Oh, secreto seguro, deleitoso!
Roto casi el navío,
a vuestro almo reposo
huyo de aqueste mar tempestuoso.
   Un no rompido sueño,
un día puro, alegre, libre quiero;
no quiero ver el ceño
vanamente severo
30 del que la sangre sube o el dinero.
   Despiértenme las aves
con su cantar süave no aprendido;
no los cuidados graves
de que es siempre seguido
quien al ajeno arbitrio está atenido.
   Vivir quiero conmigo,
gozar quiero del bien que debo al cielo,
a solas, sin testigo,
libre de amor, de celo,
40 de odio, de esperanzas, de recelo.
   Del monte en la ladera
por mi mano plantado tengo un huerto,
que con la primavera,
de bella flor cubierto,
ya muestra en esperanza el fruto cierto.
   Y como codiciosa
de ver y acrecentar su hermosura,
desde la cumbre airosa
una fontana pura
50 hasta llegar corriendo se apresura.

Y luego, sosegada,
el paso entre los árboles torciendo,
el suelo de pasada
de verdura vistiendo,
y con diversas flores va esparciendo.
    El aire el huerto orea,
y ofrece mil olores al sentido,
los árboles menea
con un manso rüido,
60   que del oro y del cetro pone olvido.
    Ténganse su tesoro
los que de un flaco leño se confían;
no es mío ver el lloro
de los que desconfían
cuando el cierzo y el ábrego porfían.
    La combatida antena
cruje, y en ciega noche el claro día
se torna; al cielo suena
confusa vocería,
70   y la mar enriquecen a porfía.
    A mí una pobrecilla
mesa, de amable paz bien abastada,
me baste; y la vajilla,
de fino oro labrada,
sea de quien la mar no teme airada.
    Y mientras miserable-
mente se están los otros abrasando
con sed insacïable
del no durable mando,
80   tendido yo a la sombra esté cantando.
    A la sombra tendido,
de hiedra y lauro eterno coronado,
puesto el atento oído
al son dulce, acordado,
del plectro sabiamente meneado.

59

A FRANCISCO SALINAS

El aire se serena
y viste de hermosura y luz no usada,
Salinas, cuando suena
la música extremada,
por vuestra sabia mano gobernada.

A cuyo son divino
mi alma, que en olvido está sumida,
torna a cobrar el tino
y memoria perdida
10 de su origen primera esclarecida.

Y como se conoce,
en suerte y pensamientos se mejora;
el oro desconoce,
que el vulgo ciego adora,
la belleza caduca, engañadora.

Traspasa el aire todo
hasta llegar a la más alta esfera,
y oye allí otro modo
de no perecedera
20 música, que es de todas la primera.

Ve cómo el gran maestro,
a aquesta inmensa cítara aplicado,
con movimiento diestro
produce el son sagrado,
con que este eterno templo es sustentado.

Y como está compuesta
de números concordes, luego envía
consonante respuesta;
y entrambas a porfía
30 mezclan una dulcísima armonía.

      Aquí la alma navega
por un mar de dulzura, y, finalmente,
en él ansí se anega,
que ningún accidente
extraño y peregrino oye o siente.
      ¡Oh, desmayo dichoso!
¡Oh, muerte que das vida! ¡Oh, dulce olvido!
¡Durase en tu reposo,
sin ser restituído
40   jamás a aqueste bajo y vil sentido!
      A aqueste bien os llamo,
gloria del apolíneo sacro coro,
amigos a quien amo
sobre todo tesoro;
que todo lo demás es triste lloro.
      ¡Oh! suene de contino,
Salinas, vuestro son en mis oídos,
por quien al bien divino
despiertan los sentidos,
50   quedando a lo demás amortecidos.

60

NOCHE SERENA

      Cuando contemplo el cielo
de innumerables luces adornado,
y miro hacia el suelo,
de noche rodeado,
en sueño y en olvido sepultado:
      el amor y la pena
despiertan en mi pecho un ansia ardiente;
despiden larga vena
los ojos hechos fuente;
10   la lengua dice al fin con voz doliente:
      "Morada de grandeza,
templo de claridad y hermosura:

mi alma que a tu alteza
nació, ¿qué desventura
la tiene en esta cárcel baja, escura?

    "¿Qué mortal desatino
de la verdad aleja ansí el sentido,
que de tu bien divino
olvidado, perdido,
20 sigue la vana sombra, el bien fingido?

    "El hombre está entregado
al sueño, de su suerte no cuidando;
y con paso callado
el cielo, vueltas dando,
las horas del vivir le va hurtando.

    "¡Ay!, despertad, mortales!
Mirad con atención en vuestro daño.
¿Las almas inmortales,
hechas a bien tamaño,
30 podrán vivir de sombra y solo engaño?

    "¡Ay!, levantad los ojos
a aquesta celestial eterna esfera:
burlaréis los antojos
de aquesa lisonjera
vida, con cuanto teme y cuanto espera.

    "¿Es más que un breve punto
el bajo y torpe suelo, comparado
a aqueste gran trasunto,
do vive mejorado
40 lo que es, lo que será, lo que ha pasado?

    "Quien mira el gran concierto
de aquestos resplandores eternales,
su movimiento cierto,
sus pasos desiguales,
y en proporción concorde tan iguales:

    "la luna cómo mueve
la plateada rueda, y va en pos de ella
la luz do el saber llueve,

y la graciosa estrella
50   de Amor la sigue reluciente y bella;
    "y cómo otro camino
prosigue el sanguinoso Marte airado,
y el Júpiter benino,
de bienes mil cercado,
serena el cielo con su rayo amado.
    "Rodéase en la cumbre
Saturno, padre de los siglos de oro;
tras dél la muchedumbre
del reluciente coro
60   su luz va repartiendo y su tesoro".
    ¿Quién es el que esto mira,
y precia la bajeza de la tierra,
y no gime, y suspira
por romper lo que encierra
el alma, y de estos bienes la destierra?
    Aquí vive el contento,
aquí reina la paz; aquí, asentado
en rico y alto asiento,
está el Amor sagrado,
70   de glorias y deleites rodeado.
    Inmensa hermosura
aquí se muestra toda, y resplandece
clarísima luz pura,
que jamás anochece:
eterna primavera aquí florece.
    ¡Oh, campos verdaderos!
¡Oh, prados con verdad dulces y amenos!
¡Riquísimos mineros!
¡Oh, deleitosos senos!
80   ¡Repuestos valles, de mil bienes llenos!

61

MORADA DEL CIELO

Alma región luciente,
prado de bienandanza, que ni al hielo
ni con el rayo ardiente
fallece: fértil suelo,
producidor eterno de consuelo.

De púrpura y de nieve
florida la cabeza coronado,
a dulces pastos mueve,
sin honda ni cayado,
10 el Buen Pastor en ti su hato amado.

Él va, y en pos dichosas
le siguen sus ovejas, do las pace
con inmortales rosas,
con flor que siempre nace,
y cuanto más se goza más renace.

Ya dentro a la montaña
del alto bien las guía; ya en la vena
del gozo fiel las baña,
y les da mesa llena,
20 pastor y pasto él solo y suerte buena.

Y de su esfera, cuando
la cumbre toca altísimo subido
el sol, él sesteando,
de su hato ceñido,
con dulce son deleita el santo oído.

Toca el rabel sonoro,
y el inmortal dulzor al alma pasa,
con que envilece el oro,
y ardiendo se traspasa;
30 y lanza en aquel bien libre de tasa.

¡Oh, son! ¡Oh, voz! Siquiera
pequeña parte alguna decendiese

en mi sentido, y fuera
de sí la alma pusiese
y toda en ti, ¡oh, Amor!, la convirtiese.
   Conocería dónde
sesteas, dulce Esposo; y desatada
de esta prisión, a donde
padece, a tu manada
40 viviré junta, sin vagar errada.

62

EN LA ASCENSIÓN

  ¡Y dejas, Pastor santo,
tu grey en este valle hondo, escuro,
con soledad y llanto!
Y tú, rompiendo el puro
aire, ¿te vas al inmortal seguro?
  Los antes bienhadados,
y los agora tristes y afligidos,
a tus pechos criados,
de Ti desposeídos,
10 ¿a dó convertirán ya sus sentidos?
  ¿Qué mirarán los ojos
que vieron de tu rostro la hermosura,
que no les sea enojos?
Quien oyó tu dulzura,
¿qué no tendrá por sordo y desventura?
  Aqueste mar turbado,
¿quién le pondrá ya freno? ¿Quién concierto
al viento fiero, airado?
Estando tú encubierto,
20 ¿qué norte guiará la nave al puerto?
  ¡Ay!, nube, envidïosa
aun de este breve gozo. ¿Qué te aquejas?
¿Dó vuelas presurosa?
¡Cuán rica tú te alejas!

¡Cuán pobres y cuán ciegos, ay, nos dejas!
   Tú llevas el tesoro,
que solo a nuestra vida enriquecía,
que desterraba el lloro,
que nos resplandecía
30 mil veces más que el puro y claro día.
   ¿Qué lazo de diamante,
¡ay, alma!, te detiene y encadena
a no seguir tu amante?
¡Ay, rompe, y sal de pena!
colócate ya libre en luz serena.
   ¿Qué temes la salida?
¿Podrá el terreno amor más que la ausencia
de tu querer y vida?
Sin cuerpo, no es violencia
40 vivir; mas lo es sin Cristo y su presencia.
   Dulce Señor y Amigo,
dulce Padre y Hermano, dulce Esposo:
en pos de Ti yo sigo,
o puesto en tenebroso
o puesto en lugar claro y glorïoso.

BALTASAR DEL ALCÁZAR
(1530–1606)

Baltasar del Alcázar was born in Seville. He served as a soldier under the Marqués de Santa Cruz and was later *alcalde* of Los Molares, near Utrera. In 1583, he returned to Seville, where he became administrator to the Conde de Gelves, the son of Herrera's patron. As a poet, he is a talented amateur whose work bears little relation to the main tendencies of his period. Luis Cernuda dismisses him as "el necio Baltasar del Alcázar". Certainly, he has none of the sobriety and concern for form one finds in his Sevillian contemporaries; his few religious poems are undistinguished, and his fame rests almost entirely on a single poem, the *Cena jocosa*, an entertaining *tour de force* whose interest is more gastronomical than literary. His favourite form is the *redondilla*, which he manages with skill and fluency; more serious claims can be made, however, for his small body of Italianate verse, which contains the two fine madrigals printed here. *Poesías*, ed. F. Rodríguez Marín, Madrid, 1910.

63

Id, suspiros ardientes,
romped el duro hielo
que ha derramado el cielo
sobre aquel corazón empedernido,
contra quien no han podido
lágrimas ni razón, amor ni ruego,
y la nieve insufrible
convertilda, suspiros, os requiero,
en otro tanto fuego;

10 pero mirad primero
no os fuerce el hielo en hielo a convertiros.
Y si esto no es posible,
suspiros, ya yo muero;
ya yo muero, suspiros.

64

Rasga la venda y mira lo que haces,
rapaz; que en esta edad no es hecho honroso
romperme el sueño y las antiguas paces;
desarma el arco, déjame en reposo,
porque la helada sangre no aprovecha,
ni es dispuesto sujeto
donde haga su efeto
la venenosa hierba de tu flecha.
Pero si determinas
10 con tus armas divinas,
rompiendo mis entrañas,
hacerme historiador de tus hazañas,
ablanda el pecho de ésta que te priva
de tu imperio y valor con su dureza,
igual a su belleza,
si no quieres, Amor, que, cuando escriba
forzado en las cadenas,
cante por tus hazañas las ajenas.

FERNANDO DE HERRERA
(1534–1597)

FERNANDO DE HERRERA spent his entire life in Seville, where he was a lay functionary of the church of San Andrés. He was a leading member of the group of writers and artists which met at the house of the Conde de Gelves, and which included the dramatist Juan de la Cueva and the historian and literary theorist Argote de Molina. Herrera's love for Doña Leonor de Millán, Condesa de Gelves, was the chief inspiration of his poetry, and the *Algunas obras* (1582), the only volume of poems published in his lifetime, was probably conceived as a tribute to her memory. Apart from his poetry, he published two short historical works, the *Relación de la guerra de Chipre y batalla naval de Lepanto* (1572) and the *Elogio de la vida y muerte de Tomás Moro* (1592), and the monumental *Obras de Garcilaso de la Vega con anotaciones de F. de H.* (1580). The enormous erudition and powers of critical judgement displayed in the *Anotaciones* place Herrera among the great poet-critics of the Renaissance; his application of systematic linguistic criteria, reflected in the scrupulous revisions of his own poems, is a crucial step in the history of Spanish verse between Garcilaso and Góngora. Herrera's love poems represent the highest and most original development of the Petrarchan tradition in Spain. Their intricate dialectic draws on many sources, from the psychological abstractions of the *cancioneros* and Ausias March to the neo-Platonic subtleties of Castiglione and Leone Hebreo; the relationship which it explores is conveyed in heroic terms, in which the woman (referred to as Luz, Lumbre, Estrella) becomes a symbol of cosmic beauty. Herrera's achievement as a love poet has been obscured until recently by the excessive praise given to his patriotic odes. These, though they share the same concept of heroism as the love poems, lack a true religious and ethical content to raise them above the level of accomplished rhetoric.

Herrera's poems exist in three collections: the *Algunas obras* (1582), the posthumous *Versos*, edited by Francisco Pacheco in 1619, and the *Rimas inéditas* (1578), recently published by Blecua. These present a difficult textual problem which is still unsolved: some poems appear differently in all three volumes, and many only exist in the 1619 text. It is now clear that this represents a later stage of composition than the *Algunas obras* of 1582. What is not clear is the extent to which Pacheco (himself a talented minor poet) revised the texts which he published. (To complicate matters, most of Herrera's manuscripts mysteriously disappeared shortly after his death.) The question is fully discussed by Macrí in his recent book (see bibliography), in which he defends the authenticity of the 1619 text against Blecua, who regards it as a mass of anomalies. Neither side has yet produced conclusive evidence, and the fact remains that the 1619 edition is the only source for a large number of Herrera's poems, including some of the finest. My own texts are taken from this edition, though for comparison I have included three versions of one of the sonnets. *Obras*, ed. V. García de Diego, *Clásicos castellanos*, vol. 26, Madrid, 1914 (The 1582 text.) *Versos*, ed. A. Coster, Strasbourg, 1914. (The 1619 text.) *Rimas inéditas*, ed. J. M. Blecua, Madrid, 1948. (Published from a MS. of 1578 in the Biblioteca Nacional, Madrid.)

65

ELEGÍA

No bañes en el mar sagrado y cano
tu estrellada corona, Noche oscura,
antes de oir este amador ufano.
    Y tú, abriendo la ʾhúmida hondura,
alza las verdes hebras de la frente,
de Náyades lozana hermosura.
    Aquí, do el grande Betis ve presente
la armada vencedora que el Egeo

con sangre coloró de Turca gente,
10   quiero decir la gloria en que me veo;
pero no cause envidia este bien mío
a quien aun no merece mi deseo.
    Sosiega el curso tuyo, insigne Río,
oye mi gloria; pues también oiste
mis quejas en tu puro asiento frío.
    Tú amaste, y como yo, también supiste
del mal dolerte y celebrar la gloria
de los pequeños bienes que tuviste.
    Corta será en mi bien la alegre historia
20   de mi favor; que corta es la alegría
que tiene algún lugar en mi memoria.
    Cuando en el claro cielo se desvía
del Sol luciente el alto carro apena,
y casi igual espacio muestra el día,
    con voz, que entre las perlas blanda suena,
teñido en puro ardor de fresca rosa,
de honesto miedo y tierno y de amor llena,
    me dijo así la bella desdeñosa
que me negaba un tiempo la esperanza,
30   sorda y dura a mi lástima llorosa:
    "Si por firmeza y dulce amar se alcanza
premio de Amor, tener yo espero y debo
de los males que sufro más holganza.
    Mil veces, por no ser ingrata, pruebo
vencer tu mucho amor, mas nunca puedo,
que es mi pecho a sentillo rudo y nuevo.
    Si en sufrir más me vences, yo te excedo
en pura fe y afetos de terneza:
vive y confía osado amante y ledo."
40   No sé si oí, si fui de su belleza
arrebatado, si perdí el sentido;
sé que allí se perdió mi fortaleza.
    Turbado dije al fin: "Por no haber sido
este sublime bien de mí esperado,

pienso que debe ser, si es bien, fingido.
   Señora, bien sabéis que mi cuidado
todo se ocupa en vos; que yo no siento,
ni pienso, sino en verme más penado.
   Mayor es que el humano mi tormento,
50 y al mayor mal igual esfuerzo tengo,
igual con el trabajo el sufrimiento.
   Las que por vos padezco y que sostengo,
penas, me dan valor, y siempre crece
mi fe, cuanto en mis males me entretengo.
   No quiero concederos que merece
mi afán tal bien, que vos probéis el daño;
más ama quien más sufre y más padece.
   No es mi pecho tan rudo o tan extraño,
que no sienta en el dulce afán primero
60 si en esto que dijistes cabe engaño.
   Armado un corazón de fuerte acero
tengo para sufrir, y está más fuerte,
cuanto más el asalto es bravo y fiero.
   Diome el Cielo la causa de esta suerte,
y yo la procuré, y hallé el camino
para poder honrarme con mi muerte."
   Lo que más entre nos pasó, no es dino,
Noche, de oir el Austro presuroso,
ni el viento de tus lechos más vecino.
70   Mete en el ancho piélago espumoso
tus luengas trenzas negras y semblante;
que en tanto que tú yaces en reposo,
podrá Amor darme gloria semejante.

66

   Vuela y cerca la lumbre y no reposa,
y huye y vuelve a su beldad rendida,
figura simple suya; y encendida
siente que fue a su muerte presurosa.

Mas yo alegre en mi luz maravillosa
a consagrar osando voy mi vida,
que espera, de su bello ardor vencida,
o perderse o cobrarse venturosa.
　　Amor, que en mí engrandece su memoria,
10　entibia mi esperanza en lento engaño,
y en llama ingrata ufano me consumo.
　　Cuidé (¡tal fue mi mal!) ganar la gloria
del bien que vi, y al fin hallo en mi daño
que solo de mi incendio resta el humo.

67

Dulce el fuego de Amor, dulce la pena,
y dulce de mi daño es la memoria,
cuando renueva Amor la antigua historia
que a su grave tormento me condena.
　　Mas cuando hallo mi esperanza llena
de bien y de promesas de vitoria,
un súbito dolor turba mi gloria,
y todos mis contentos desordena.
　　Que será esta Luz pura de belleza,
10　la fe del justo Amor, en poca tierra
vuelta, y el fuego muerto que me inflama.
　　¡Oh vano ardor de la mortal flaqueza,
si el fin que ofrece paz de tanta guerra
no dejará aun ceniza de mi llama!

68

Alma, que ya en la luz del puro cielo
ardes de santo fuego; a quien suspira
tu ausencia, con süaves ojos mira,
y alienta a levantar el flaco vuelo.
　　Ceñida en torno tú de rojo velo,
la llama en mi lloroso pecho inspira;

porque sin odio, sin temor, sin ira
desprecie el vano amor y error del suelo.
   Lloré yo tu partida, amé tu gloria,
10 y en tu último dolor creció mi pena
para seguir contigo el mesmo hado.
   Si la fe te renueva la memoria,
en esta sombra ven con faz serena
a consolar el corazón cuitado.

69

   Ahora que cubrió de blanco hielo
el oro la hermosa Aurora mía,
blanco es el puro Sol, y blanco el día,
y blanco el color lúcido del cielo,
   blancas todas tus viras que recelo;
es blanco el arco y rayos de alegría,
Amor, con que me hieres a porfía,
blanco tu ardiente fuego y frío hielo.
   Mas ¿qué puedo esperar desta blancura,
10 pues tiene en blanca nieve el pecho tierno
contra mi fiera llama defendido?
   ¡Oh Beldad sin amor, oh mi Ventura!,
que abrasado en vigor de fuego eterno,
muero en un blanco hielo convertido.

70

   Amor, en un incendio no acabado
ardí del fuego tuyo, en la florida
sazón y alegre de mi dulce vida,
todo en tu viva imagen trasformado.
   Y ahora (oh vano error) en este estado,
no con llama en cenizas ascondida,
mas descubierta, clara y encendida,
pierdo en ti lo mejor de mi cuidado.

No más, baste, crüel, ya en tantos años
10   rendido haber al yugo el cuello yerto,
y haber visto en el fin tu desvarío.
   Abra la luz la niebla a tus engaños,
antes que el lazo rompa el tiempo, y muerto
sea el fuego del tardo hielo mío.

71

(1578 *version*)

   Rojo sol, que con llama glorïosa
das color al profundo y alto cielo,
¿hallaste tal belleza en todo el suelo
que igualase a mi bella Luz dichosa?
   Aura süave, blanda y amorosa,
que nos regalas con el fresco vuelo,
cuando se cubre del dorado velo
mi Luz, ¿tocaste trenza más hermosa?
   Luna, honor de la noche, ilustre coro
10   de las errantes formas y fijadas,
¿considerastes tales dos estrellas?
   Sol puro, Aura, Luna, luces de oro,
¿oistes vos mis penas nunca usadas?
¿Vistes Luz más ingrata a mis querellas?

72

(1582 *version*)

   Rojo sol, que con hacha luminosa
coloras el purpúreo y alto cielo,
¿hallaste tal belleza en todo el suelo
que iguale a mi serena Luz dichosa?
   Aura süave, blanda y amorosa,
que nos halagas con tu fresco vuelo,
cuando se cubre del dorado velo
mi Luz, ¿tocaste trenza más hermosa?

Luna, honor de la noche, ilustre coro
10 de las errantes lumbres y fijadas,
¿considerastes tales dos estrellas?
   Sol puro, Aura, Luna, llamas de oro,
¿oistes vos mis penas nunca usadas?
¿vistes Luz más ingrata a mis querellas?

73

(1619 version)

Rojo sol, que con hacha luminosa
coloras el purpúreo y alto cielo,
¿hallaste tal belleza en todo el suelo
que iguale a mi serena Luz dichosa?
   Aura süave, blanda y amorosa,
que nos halagas con tu fresco vuelo,
cuando el oro descubre y rico velo
mi Luz, ¿trenza tocaste más hermosa?
   Luna, honor de la noche, ilustre coro
10 de los errantes astros y fijados,
¿considerastes tales dos estrellas?
   Sol puro, Aura, Luna, luces de oro,
¿oistes mis dolores nunca usados?
¿vistes Luz más ingrata a mis querellas?

74

POR LA PÉRDIDA DEL REY DON SEBASTIÁN

Voz de dolor y canto de gemido
y espíritu de miedo, envuelto en ira,
hagan principio acerbo a la memoria
de aquel día fatal aborrecido
que Lusitania mísera suspira,
desnuda de valor, falta de gloria;
y la llorosa historia
asombre con horror funesto y triste

dende el áfrico Atlante y seno ardiente
10   hasta do el mar de otro color se viste,
y do el límite rojo de Orïente,
y todas sus vencidas gentes fieras
ven tremolar de Cristo las banderas.
     ¡Ay de los que pasaron, confïados
en sus caballos y en la muchedumbre
de sus carros, en ti, Libia desierta,
y en su vigor y fuerzas engañados,
no alzaron su esperanza a aquella cumbre
de eterna luz; mas con soberbia cierta
20   se ofrecieron la incierta
vitoria; y sin volver a Dios sus ojos,
con yerto cuello y corazón ufano
sólo atendieron siempre a los despojos!
Y el santo de Israel abrió su mano,
y los dejó, y cayó en despeñadero
el carro y el caballo y caballero.
     Vino el día crüel, el día lleno
de indinación, de ira y furor, que puso
en soledad y en un profundo llanto
30   de gente y de placer el reino ajeno.
El cielo no alumbró, quedó confuso
el nuevo sol, presago de mal tanto;
y con terrible espanto
el Señor visitó sobre sus males,
para humillar los fuertes arrogantes,
y levantó los bárbaros no iguales,
que con osados pechos y constantes
no busquen oro, mas con hierro airado
la ofensa venguen y el error culpado.
40   Los ímpios y robustos, indinados,
las ardientes espadas desnudaron
sobre la claridad y hermosura
de tu gloria y valor, y no cansados
en tu muerte, tu honor todo afearon,

mesquina Lusitania sin ventura;
y con frente segura
rompieron sin temor con fiero estrago
tus armadas escuadras y braveza.
La arena se tornó sangriento lago,
50 la llanura con muertes, aspereza;
cayó en unos vigor, cayó denuedo,
mas en otros, desmayo y torpe miedo.

   ¿Son éstos, por ventura, los famosos,
los fuertes, los belígeros varones
que conturbaron con furor la tierra,
que sacudieron reinos poderosos,
que domaron las hórridas naciones,
que pusieron desierto en cruda guerra
cuanto el mar Indo encierra,
60 y soberbias ciudades destruyeron?
¿Dó el corazón seguro y la osadía?
¿Cómo así se acabaron y perdieron
tanto heroico valor en sólo un día;
y lejos de su patria derribados,
no fueron justamente sepultados?

   Tales ya fueron éstos, cual hermoso
cedro del alto Líbano, vestido
de ramos, hojas con ecelsa alteza;
las aguas lo criaron poderoso,
70 sobre empinados árboles crecido,
y se multiplicaron en grandeza
sus ramos con belleza
y, extendiendo su sombra, se anidaron
las aves que sustenta el grande cielo,
y en sus hojas las fieras engendraron,
y hizo a mucha gente umbroso velo:
no igualó en celsitud y hermosura
jamás árbol alguno a su figura.
   Pero elevóse con su verde cima,
80 y sublimó la presunción su pecho,

desvanecido todo y confïado,
haciendo de su alteza sólo estima.
Por eso Dios lo derribó deshecho,
a los ímpios y ajenos entregado,
por la raíz cortado;
que opreso de los montes arrojados,
sin ramos y sin hojas y desnudo,
huyeron dél los hombres espantados,
que su sombra tuvieron por escudo;
90   en su rüina y ramos cuantas fueron
las aves y las fieras se pusieron.

    Tú, infanda Libia, en cuya seca arena
murió el vencido reino Lusitano,
y se acabó su generosa gloria,
no estés alegre y de ufanía llena,
porque tu temerosa y flaca mano
hubo sin esperarla tal vitoria,
indina de memoria;
que si el justo dolor mueve a venganza
100   alguna vez el español coraje,
despedazada con aguda lanza
compensarás muriendo el hecho ultraje;
y Luco, amedrentado, al mar inmenso
pagará de africana sangre el censo.

FRANCISCO DE FIGUEROA
(1536–1617?)

FRANCISCO DE FIGUEROA was born in Alcalá de Henares. He studied
and soldiered in Italy, and in 1579 went to Flanders in the service
of Don Carlos de Aragón, Duque de Terranova. His last years
were spent in Alcalá. Shortly before his death he gave orders for
his poems to be destroyed; those which survived were published in
1626. Figueroa wrote poetry in both Italian and Spanish and is
notable for his experiments in blank verse. His chief influences are
Garcilaso and Petrarch, though many of his best poems are genuine
re-creations. No model is known for either of the sonnets I have
included; the second of these shows his gift for replacing stock
comparisons by fresh, sensual imagery. *Poesías*, ed. A. González
Palencia, Madrid, 1943.

75

Partiendo de la luz, donde solía
venir su luz, mis ojos han cegado:
perdió también el corazón cuitado
el precioso manjar de que vivía.
El alma desechó la compañía
del cuerpo, y fuése tras el rostro amado;
así en mi triste ausencia he siempre estado
ciego y con hambre y sin el alma mía.
Agora que al lugar, que el pensamiento
10   nunca dejó, mis pasos presurosos
después de mil trabajos me han traído,
cobraron luz mis ojos tenebrosos
y su pastura el corazón hambriento,
pero no tornará el alma a su nido.

76

Quien ve las blancas y hermosas rosas
de mano virginal recién cogidas,
y con diversos tallos retejidas,
guirnaldas bellas hacen y olorosas;
   quien gusta de las aves más preciosas
las tiernas pechuguillas convertidas
en líquidos, manjares y comidas
süaves, odoríferas, sabrosas;
   y quien panales albos destilando
10 la rubia miel de la amarilla cera,
a lo que al gusto y vista más provoca,
   pues tal es de mi ninfa el rostro, cuando
mi vista de la suya reverbera
y bebo las palabras de su boca.

FRANCISCO DE ALDANA
(1537–1578)

THE parents of Francisco de Aldana came from Extremadura, though he himself was probably born in Naples, where his father was a professional soldier. In 1540, his family settled in Florence, under the protection of Cosimo de' Medici. Aldana grew up in the atmosphere of Florentine neo-Platonism, of which there are many traces in his work. In 1567 he entered the service of the Duque de Alba, at that time Governor of the Netherlands; he fought in a number of campaigns and was seriously wounded at the siege of Alkmaar (1573). Aldana visited Spain for the first time in 1571, and returned there permanently five years later. He had a high reputation as a soldier and an adviser on military affairs; shortly after his appointment as Governor of the fortress of San Sebastián, he was sent as a government spy to North Africa in order to obtain information which might dissuade the young King Sebastian of Portugal from his plans for an African invasion. The king, how-ever, was more impressed by Aldana's personal qualities than by his warnings of Moorish military strength, and obtained permission from Philip II for Aldana to accompany him as Commander of the Portuguese army. Aldana, like Sebastian himself, was killed in the disaster of Alcázarquivir. (See Herrera's ode on this event, p. 105.) Aldana's best poems have an intellectual concentration and a wealth of vivid concrete imagery which place him among the major poets of his period. His combination of Renaissance human-ism and Christian belief suggests parallels with Luis de León, with whom he shares an intense wish for mystical experience, expressed in neo-Platonic terms. The verse letter to the humanist Arias Montano, written less than a year before his death, is one of the greatest poetic meditations in the language. His most recent editor calls it "una epístola horaciana a lo divino"; the interplay between metrical structure and natural speech rhythms is the driving force behind even the most intensely metaphysical passages of the poem. *Poesías*, ed. E. L. Rivers, *Clásicos castellanos*, vol. 143, Madrid, 1957.

77

Mil veces callo que romper deseo
el cielo a gritos, y otras tantas tiento
dar a mi lengua voz y movimiento,
que en silencio mortal yacer la veo;
   anda cual velocísimo correo
por dentro al alma el suelto pensamiento
con alto y de dolor lloroso acento,
casi en sombra de muerte un nuevo Orfeo.
   No halla la memoria o la esperanza
10 rastro de imagen dulce y deleitable
con que la voluntad viva segura:
   cuanto en mí hallo es maldición que alcanza,
muerte que tarda, llanto inconsolable,
desdén del Cielo, error de la ventura.

78

RECONOCIMIENTO DE LA VANIDAD DEL MUNDO

En fin, en fin, tras tanto andar muriendo,
tras tanto varïar vida y destino,
tras tanto de uno en otro desatino
pensar todo apretar, nada cogiendo,
   tras tanto acá y allá yendo y viniendo
cual sin aliento inútil peregrino,
¡oh Dios!, tras tanto error del buen camino,
yo mismo de mi mal ministro siendo,
   hallo, en fin, que ser muerto en la memoria
10 del mundo es lo mejor que en él se asconde,
pues es la paga dél muerte y olvido,

y en un rincón vivir con la vitoria
de sí, puesto el querer tan sólo adonde
es premio el mismo Dios de lo servido.

79

CARTA DEL CAPITÁN FRANCISCO DE ALDANA PARA ARIAS MONTANO SOBRE LA CONTEMPLACIÓN DE DIOS Y LOS REQUISITOS DELLA

Montano, cuyo nombre es la primera
estrellada señal por do camina
el Sol el cerco oblicuo de la esfera,
   nombrado así por voluntad divina
para mostrar que en ti comienza Apolo
la luz de su celeste disciplina:
   yo soy un hombre desvalido y solo,
expuesto al duro hado cual marchita
hoja al rigor del descortés Eolo;
10   mi vida temporal anda precita
dentro el infierno del común trafago
que siempre añade un mal y un bien nos quita.
   Oficio militar profeso y hago,
¡baja condenación de mi ventura!,
que al alma dos infiernos da por pago:
   los huesos y la sangre que Natura
me dio para vivir, no poca parte
dellos y della he dado a la locura,
   mientras el pecho al desenvuelto Marte
20   tan libre di que sin mi daño puede,
hablando la verdad, ser muda el arte;
   y el rico galardón que se concede
a mi (llámola así) ciega porfía
es que por ciego y porfïado quede.
   No digo más sobre esto, que podría
cosas decir que un mármol deshiciese

en el piadoso humor que el ojo envía,
  y callaré las causas de interese
(no sé si justo o injusto) que en alguno
30 hubo porque mi mal más largo fuese;
  menos te quiero ser ora importuno
en declarar mi vida y nacimiento,
que tiempo dará Dios más oportuno:
  basta decir que cuatro veces ciento
y dos cuarenta vueltas dadas miro
del planeta septeno al firmamento
  que en el aire común vivo y respiro
sin haber hecho más que andar haciendo
yo mismo a mí crüel, doblado tiro
40 y con un trasgo a brazos debatiendo
que al cabo, al cabo, ¡ay Dios!, de tan gran rato
mi costoso sudor queda rïendo.
  Mas ya, ¡merced del Cielo!, me desato,
ya rompo a la esperanza lisonjera
el lazo en que me asió con doble trato:
  pienso torcer de la común carrera
que sigue el vulgo y caminar derecho
jornada de mi patria verdadera;
  entrarme en el secreto de mi pecho
50 y platicar en él mi interior hombre,
dó va, dó está, si vive, o qué se ha hecho.
  Y porque vano error más no me asombre,
en algún alto y solitario nido
pienso enterrar mi ser, mi vida y nombre
  y, como si no hubiera acá nacido,
estarme allá, cual Eco, replicando
al dulce son de Dios, del alma oído.
  Y ¿qué debiera ser, bien contemplando,
el alma sino un eco resonante
60 a la eterna Beldad que está llamando
  y, desde el cavernoso y vacilante
cuerpo, volver mis réplicas de amores

al sobrecelestial Narciso amante;
   rica de sus intrínsicos favores,
con un piadoso escarnio el bajo oficio
burlar de los mundanos amadores?
   En tierra o en árbol hoja algún bullicio
no hace que, al moverse, ella no encuentra
en nuevo y para Dios grato ejercicio;
70   y como el fuego saca y desencentra
oloroso licor por alquitara
del cuerpo de la rosa que en ella entra,
   así destilará, de la gran cara
del mundo, inmaterial varia belleza
con el fuego de amor que la prepara;
   y pasará de vuelo a tanta alteza
que, volviéndose a ver tan sublimada,
su misma olvidará naturaleza,
   cuya capacidad ya dilatada
80 allá verá do casi ser le toca
en su primera Causa transformada.
   Ojos, oídos, pies, manos y boca,
hablando, obrando, andando, oyendo y viendo,
serán del mar de Dios cubierta roca;
   cual pece dentro el vaso alto, estupendo,
del Océano irá su pensamiento
desde Dios para Dios yendo y viniendo:
   seróle allí quietud el movimiento,
cual círculo mental sobre el divino
90 centro, glorioso origen del contento;
   que, pues el alto, esférico, camino
del cielo causa en él vida y holganza
sin que lugar adquiera peregrino,
   llegada el alma al fin de la esperanza,
mejor se moverá para quietarse
dentro el lugar que sobre el mundo alcanza,
   do llega en tanto extremo a mejorarse
(torno a decir) que en él se transfigura,

casi el velo mortal sin animarse:
100 no que del alma la especial natura,
dentro al divino piélago hundida,
cese en el Hacedor de ser hechura
     o quede aniquilada y destrüida
cual gota de licor que el rostro enciende,
del altísimo mar toda absorbida,
     mas como el aire, en quien en luz se extiende
el claro sol, que juntos aire y lumbre
ser una misma cosa el ojo entiende.
     Es bien verdad que a tan sublime cumbre
110 suele impedir el venturoso vuelo
del cuerpo la terrena pesadumbre,
     pero, con todo, llega al bajo suelo
la escala de Jacob, por do podemos
al alcázar subir del alto cielo,
     que, yendo allá, no dudo que encontremos
favor de más de un ángel diligente
con quien alegre tránsito llevemos.
     Puede del sol pequeña fuerza ardiente
desde la tierra alzar graves vapores
120 a la región del aire allá eminente,
     ¿y tantos celestiales protectores,
para subir a Dios alma sencilla,
vernán a ejercitar fuerzas menores?
     Mas pues, Montano, va mi navecilla
corriendo este gran mar con suelta vela
hacia la infinidad buscando orilla,
     quiero, para tejer tan rica tela,
muy desde atrás decir lo que podría
hacer el alma que a su causa vuela.
130   Paréceme, Montano, que debría
buscar lugar que al dulce pensamiento,
encaminado a Dios, abra la vía,
     adó todo exterior derramamiento
cese, y en su secreto el alma entrada

comience a examinar con modo atento,
    antes que del Señor fuese crïada,
cómo no fue ni pudo haber salido
de aquella privación que llaman nada;
    ver aquel alto piélago de olvido,
140 aquel sin hacer pie luengo vacío,
tomado tan atrás del no haber sido;
    y diga a Dios: "¡Oh Causa del ser mío,
cuál me sacaste desa muerte escura,
rica del don de vida y de albedrío!"
    Allí, gozosa en la mayor natura,
déjese el alma andar süavemente
con leda admiración de su ventura;
    húndase toda en la divina fuente
y, del vital licor humedecida,
150 sálgase a ver del tiempo en la corriente:
    veráse como línea producida
del punto eterno, en el mortal sujeto
bajada a gobernar la humana vida
    dentro la cárcel del corpóreo afeto,
hecha horizonte allí deste alterable
mundo y del puro y sin defeto;
    donde, a su fin únicamente amable
vuelta, conozca del ser tan dichosa
forma gentil de vida indeclinable
160   y sienta que la mano dadivosa
de Dios cosas crïó tantas y tales,
hasta la más süez, mínima cosa,
    sin que las calidades principales,
los cielos con su lúcida belleza,
los coros del Impíreo angelicales
    consigan facultad de tanta alteza
que lo más bajo y vil que asconde el cieno
puedan crïar, ni hay tal naturaleza.
    Enamórese el alma en ver cuán bueno
170 es Dios, que un gusanillo le podría

llamar su crïador de lleno en lleno,
  y poco a poco le amanezca el día
de la contemplación, siempre cobrando
luz y calor que Dios de allá le envía.
  Déjese descansar de cuando en cuando
sin procurar subir, porque no rompa
el hilo que el amor queda tramando,
  y veráse colmar de alegre pompa,
de divino favor tan ordenado
180 cuan libre de desmán que le interrompa.
  Torno a decir que el pecho enamorado
la celestial, de allá, rica inflüencia
espere humilde, atento y reposado,
  sin dar ni recibir propia sentencia,
que en tal lugar la lengua más despierta
es de natura error y balbucencia.
  Abra de par en par la firme puerta
de su querer, pues no tan presto pasa
el sol por la región del aire abierta
190 ni el agua universal con menos tasa
hinchió toda del suelo alta abertura,
bajando a la región de luz escasa,
  como aquella mayor, suma Natura
hinche de su divino sentimiento
el alma cuando abrírsele procura.
  No que de allí le quede atrevimiento
para creer que en sí mérito encierra
con que al Supremo obligue entendimiento,
  pues la impotencia misma que la tierra
200 tiene para obligar que le dé el cielo
llovida ambrosia en valle, en llano, o en sierra,
  o para producir flores el hielo
y plantas levantar de verde cima
desierto estéril y arenoso suelo,
  tiene el alma mejor, de más estima,
para obligar que en ella gracia influya

el bien que a tanta alteza la sublima:
   es don de Dios, magnificencia suya,
divina autoridad que el ser abona,
210 de nuestra indignidad que no le arguya,
   y cuando da de gloria la corona,
es último favor que los ya hechos,
como sus propios méritos, corona.
   Así, que el alma en los divinos pechos
beba infusión de gracia sin buscalla,
sin gana de sentir nuevos provechos,
   que allí la dilligencia menos halla
cuanto más busca, y suelen los favores
trocarse en interior, nueva batalla.
220 No tiene que buscar los resplandores
del sol quien de su luz anda cercado,
ni el rico abril pedir hierbas y flores;
   pues no mejor el húmido pescado
dentro del abismo está del Oceano
cubierto del humor grave y salado
   que el alma, alzado sobre el curso humano,
queda, sin ser curiosa o diligente,
de aquel gran mar cubierta ultramundano,
   no, como el pece, sólo exteriormente,
230 mas dentro mucho más que esté en el fuego
el íntimo calor que en él se siente.
   Digo que, puesta el alma en su sosiego,
espere a Dios cual ojo que cayendo
se va sabrosamente al sueño ciego,
   que al que trabaja por quedar durmiendo,
esa misma inquietud destrama el hilo
del sueño, que se da no le pidiendo;
   ella verá con desusado estilo
toda regarse, y regalarse junto,
240 de un salido de Dios sagrado Nilo;
   recogida su luz toda en un punto,
a Aquélla mirará de quien es ella

indignamente imagen y trasunto
    y, cual de amor la matutina estrella
dentro el abismo del eterno día,
se cubrirá toda luciente y bella.
    Como la hermosísima judía
que, llena de doncel, novicio, espanto
viendo Isaac que para sí venía,
250   dejó cubrir el rostro con el manto
y, descendida presto del camello,
recoge humilde al novio casto y santo:
    disponga el alma así con Dios hacello
y de su presunción descienda altiva,
cubierto el rostro y reclinado el cuello,
    y a aquella sacrosanta virtud viva,
única, crïadora y redemptora,
con profunda humildad en sí reciba.
    Mas ¿quién dirá, mas quién decir agora
260 podrá los peregrinos sentimientos
que el alma en sus potencias atesora?:
    aquellos ricos amontonamientos
de sobrecelestiales inflüencias,
dilatados de amor descubrimientos;
    aquellas ilustradas advertencias
de las musas de Dios sobreesenciales,
destierro general de contingencias;
    aquellos nutrimentos divinales,
de la inmortalidad fomentadores,
270 que exceden los posibles naturales;
    aquellos, ¿qué diré?, colmos favores,
privanzas nunca oídas, nunca vistas,
suma especialidad del bien de amores.
    ¡Oh grandes, oh riquísimas conquistas
de las Indias de Dios, de aquel gran mundo
tan escondido a las mundanas vistas!
    Mas ¡ay de mí!, que voy hacia el profundo
do no se entiende suelo ni ribera,

y si no vuelvo atrás, me anego y hundo.
280   No más allá. Ni puedo, aunque lo quiera.
Do la vista alcanzó, llegó la mano;
ya se les cierra a entrambos la carrera.
     ¿Notaste bien, doctísimo Montano,
notaste cuál salí, más atrevido
que del cretense padre el hijo insano?
     Tratar en esto es sólo a ti debido,
en quien el Cielo sus noticias llueve
para dejar el mundo enriquecido;
     por quien de Pindo las hermanas nueve
290 dejan sus montes, dejan sus amadas
aguas, donde la sed se mata y bebe,
     y en el santo Sïón ya trasladadas,
al profético coro por tu boca
oyendo están, atentas y humilladas.
     ¡Dichosísimo aquél que estar le toca
contigo en bosque o en monte o en valle umbroso
o encima la más alta áspera roca!
     ¡Oh tres y cuatro veces yo dichoso
si fuese Aldino aquél, si aquél yo fuese,
300 que en orden de vivir tan venturoso
     juntamente contigo estar pudiese,
lejos de error, de engaño y sobresalto,
como si el mundo en sí no me incluyese!
     Un monte dicen que hay sublime y alto,
tanto que, al parecer, la excelsa cima
al cielo muestra dar glorioso asalto
     y que el pastor con su ganado encima
debajo de sus pies correr el trueno
ve dentro el nubiloso, helado clima,
310   y en el puro, vital aire sereno
va respirando allá, libre y exento,
casi nuevo lugar, del mundo ajeno,
     sin que le impida el desmandado viento,
el trabado granizo, el suelto rayo,

    ni el de la tierra grueso, húmido aliento:
      todo es tranquilidad de fértil mayo,
    purísima del sol templada lumbre,
    de hielo o de calor sin triste ensayo.
      Pareces tú, Montano, a la gran cumbre
320   deste gran monte, pues vivir contigo
    es muerte de la misma pesadumbre,
      es un poner debajo a su enemigo:
    de la soberbia el trueno estar mirando
    cuál va descomponiendo al más amigo;
      las nubes de la invidia descargando
    ver de murmuración duro granizo,
    de vanagloria el viento andar soplando,
      y de lujuria el rayo encontradizo,
    de acidia el grueso aliento y de avaricia,
330   con lo demás que el padre antiguo hizo;
      y desta turba vil que el mundo envicia
    descargado, gozar cuanto ilustrare
    el sol en ti de gloria y de justicia.
      El alma que contigo se juntare
    cierto reprimirá cualquier deseo
    que contra el proprio bien la vida encare;
      podrá luchar con el terrestre Anteo
    de su rebelde cuerpo, aunque le cueste
    vencer la lid por fuerza y por rodeo,
340   y casi vuelta un Hércules celeste,
    sompesará de tierra ese imperfeto,
    porque el favor no pase della en éste,
      tanto que el pie del sensitivo afeto
    no la llegue a tocar y el enemigo
    al hercúleo valor quede sujeto;
      de sí le apartará, junto consigo
    domándole, firmado en la potencia
    del pecho ejecutor del gran castigo;
      serán temor de Dios y penitencia
350   los brazos, coronada de diadema

la caridad, valor de toda esencia.
    Mas para conclüir tan largo tema,
quiero el lugar pintar do, con Montano,
deseo llegar de vida al hora extrema.
    No busco monte excelso y soberano
de ventiscosa cumbre en quien se halle
la triplicada nieve en el verano;
    menos profundo, escuro, húmido valle
donde las aguas bajan despeñadas
360 por entre desigual, torcida calle:
    las partes medias son más aprobadas
de la natura, siempre fructüosas,
siempre de nuevas flores esmaltadas.
    Quiero también, Montano, entre otras cosas,
no lejos descubrir de nuestro nido
el alto mar, con ondas bulliciosas:
    dos elementos ver, uno movido
del aéreo desdén, otro fijado
sobre su mismo peso establecido;
370   ver uno desigual, otro igualado,
de mil colores éste, aquél mostrando
el claro azul del cielo no añublado.
    Bajaremos allá de cuando en cuando,
altas y ponderadas maravillas
en recíproco amor juntos tratando;
    verás por las marítimas orillas
la espumosa resaca entre el arena
bruñir mil blancas conchas y lucillas;
    en quien hiriendo el sol con luz serena,
380 echan como de sí nuevos resoles
do el rayo visüal su curso enfrena.
    Verás mil retorcidas caracoles,
mil bucios estriados, con señales
y pintas de lustrosas arreboles:
    los unos del color de los corales,
los otros de la luz que el sol represa

en los pintados arcos celestiales,
  de varia operación, de varia empresa,
despidiendo de sí como centellas,
390 en rica mezcla de oro y de turquesa.
  Cualquiera especie producir de aquéllas
verás (lo que en la tierra no acontece)
pequeñas en extremo y grandes dellas,
  donde el secreto, artificioso pece
pegado está y, en otros, despegarse
suele y al mar salir, si le parece;
  por cierto, cosa digna de admirarse
tan menudo animal sin niervo y hueso
encima tan gran máquina arrastrarse,
400 crïar el agua un cuerpo tan espeso
como la concha, casi fuerte muro
reparador de todo caso avieso,
  todo de fuera peñascoso y duro,
liso de dentro, que al salir injuria
no haga su señor tratable y puro;
  el nácar, el almeja y la purpuria
vénera, con matices luminosos
que acá y allá del mar siguen la furia,
  ver los marinos riscos cavernosos
410 por alto y bajo en varia forma abiertos,
do encuentran mil embates espumosos,
  los peces acudir por sus inciertos
caminos con agalla purpurina,
de escamoso cristal todos cubiertos.
  También verás correr por la marina,
con sus airosas tocas, sesga y presta,
la nave, a lejos climas peregrina;
  verás encaramar la comba cresta
del líquido elemento a los extremos
420 de la helada región, al fuego opuesta.
  Los salados abismos miraremos
entre dos sierras de agua abrir cañada,

que de temor Carón suelta sus remos.
   Veráse luego mansa y reposada
la mar, que por sirena nos figura
la bien régida y sabia edad pasada,
   la cual en tan gentil, blanda postura
vista del marinero, se adormece
casi a música voz, süave y pura,
430   y en tanto el fiero mar se arbola y crece
de modo que, aun despierto, ya cualquiera
remedio de vivir le desfallece.
   En fin, Montano, el que temiendo espera
y velando ama, sólo éste prevale
en la estrecha, de Dios, cierta carrera.
   Mas ya parece que mi pluma sale
del término de epístola, escribiendo
a ti, que eres de mí lo que más vale:
   a mayor ocasión voy remitiendo
440 de nuestra soledad contemplativa
algún nuevo primor que della entiendo.
   Tú, mi Montano, así tu Aldino viva
contigo en paz dichosa esto que queda
por consumir de vida fugitiva
   y el Cielo cuanto pides te conceda,
que nunca de su todo se desmiembre
esta tu parte y siempre serlo pueda.
   Nuestro Señor en ti su gracia siembre
para coger la gloria que promete.
450 De Madrid a los siete de setiembre,
mil y quinientos y setenta y siete.

FRANCISCO DE LA TORRE

Nothing is known of Francisco de la Torre, whose poems were first published by Quevedo in 1631. Their models, and the simple elegance of their style, suggest a poet writing in the 1560s and '70s. His *Endechas* in six-syllable quatrains, though not among his best poems, are an interesting survival of an older metre. The rest of his work is in Italianate forms—sonnets, odes, *canciones* and eclogues; the quiet melancholy of his sonnets to night is very distinctive, and shows a curiously romantic sensibility. The short ode which I have included is a remarkably fresh version of a theme—"Collige, virgo, rosas"—handled by dozens of sixteenth-century poets. *Poesías*, ed. A. Zamora Vicente, *Clásicos castellanos*, vol. 124, Madrid, 1944.

80

Mira, Filis, furiosa
onda, que sigue y huye la ribera
y torna presurosa,
echando al punto fuera
del agua el peso de la nao ligera.
  Aquellas despojadas
plantas, que son estériles abrojos,
solían adornadas
de cárdenos y rojos
10 ramos, lucir ante tus bellos ojos.
  Vino del Austro frío
invierno yerto y abrasó la hermosa
gloria del valle umbrío
y derribó la hojosa
corona de los árboles umbrosa.

Agora que el Oriente
de tu belleza reverbera, agora
que el rayo transparente
de la rosada Aurora
20 abre tus ojos y tu frente dora,
    antes que la dorada
cumbre de relucientes llamas de oro
húmida y argentada
quede, inútil tesoro
consagrado al errante y fijo coro,
    goza, Filis, del aura
que la concha de Venus hiere; dado
que apenas se restaura
el contento pasado,
30 como el día de ayer y el no gozado.
    Vendrá la temerosa
noche de nieblas y de vientos llena,
marchitará la rosa
purpúrea y la azucena
nevada mustia tornará de amena.

81

Sigo, silencio, tu estrellado manto,
de transparentes lumbres guarnecido,
enemiga del Sol esclarecido,
ave nocturna de agorero canto.
    El falso mago Amor, con el encanto
de palabras quebradas por olvido,
convirtió mi razón y mi sentido,
mi cuerpo no, por deshacelle en llanto.
    Tú, que sabes mi mal, y tú, que fuiste
10 la ocasión principal de mi tormento,
por quien fui venturoso y desdichado,
    oye tú solo mi dolor, que al triste
a quien persigue cielo violento,
no le está bien que sepa su cuidado.

82

¡Cuántas veces te me has engalanado,
clara y amiga noche! ¡Cuántas, llena
de escuridad y espanto, la serena
mansedumbre del cielo me has turbado!
Estrellas hay que saben mi cuidado
y que se han regalado con mi pena;
que, entre tanta beldad, la más ajena
de amor tiene su pecho enamorado.
Ellas saben amar, y saben ellas
10 que he contado su mal llorando el mío,
envuelto en los dobleces de tu manto.
Tú, con mil ojos, noche, mis querellas
oye y esconde, pues mi amargo llanto
es fruto inútil que al amor envío.

PEDRO LAYNEZ
(c. 1538–1584)

PEDRO LAYNEZ is best known as a friend of Cervantes, Montemayor, Figueroa, Espinel and other writers. He was a talented minor poet, working in both Italianate and traditional forms. Fucilla calls him "poeta por excelencia del desengaño y de la ausencia". The two sonnets printed here have an intensity and an economy of phrasing which he seldom achieves in his other poems. The second is a partial imitation of Camoens's sonnet "Lembranças, que lembrais o bem passado". *Obras*, ed. J. de Entrambasaguas, 2 vols., Madrid, 1951.

83

Salga con la doliente ánima fuera
la dolorosa voz sin alegría,
busque mi grave llanto nueva vía,
llorando pena tan amarga y fiera;
　　cámbiese ya mi alegre primavera
en noche eternamente escura y fría,
y pues muero por ti, señora mía,
escucha mi cansada voz postrera.
　　No muero desamado ni celoso,
10　que igual es cualquier suerte en tu presencia,
sólo un dolor me acaba agudo y fiero.
　　Para encubrirle más, ya no hay paciencia,
para mostrar cuál es, soy temeroso;
en fin, es tal que por callarle muero.

84

Memorias tristes del placer pasado,
vivas espuelas del dolor presente,
pues presto he de morir estando ausente,
no me acordéis el bien que es ya acabado.
    Porque para matarme es excusado,
sobre ausencia, juntar nuevo accidente;
de ausencia moriré, de fuego ardiente
bien presto consumido y abrasado.
    Mas, ¡ay tristes memorias!, no hay reparo
10 al daño que me hace la memoria,
el cual no siento por perder la vida,
    sino por acordarme, ¡ay cielo avaro!,
que la dulce, pasada, breve gloria
que yo perdí, de otro es poseída.

GASPAR GIL POLO
(d. 1585)

Little is known of the Valencian writer Gil Polo, author of the pastoral novel *La Diana enamorada* (1564), though some scholars have identified him with a Professor of Greek of the same name who taught at the University of Valencia between 1565 and 1574. Apart from a few dedicatory sonnets, his entire poetic work is contained in the verse interludes of his novel. The dominant influence is Garcilaso, but Gil Polo experiments successfully in a variety of metrical patterns, both traditional and Italianate. His writing has great technical assurance and sense of form, and occasionally, as in the sonnet printed here, a note of genuine feeling which rises above the fictional context. *La Diana enamorada*, ed. R. Ferreres, *Clásicos castellanos*, vol. 135, Madrid, 1953.

85

Cuando la brava ausencia un alma hiere,
se ceba, imaginando el pensamiento
que el bien que está más lejos, más contento
el corazón hará cuando viniere.

Remedio hay al dolor de quien tuviere
en esperanza puesto el fundamento,
que al fin tiene algún premio del tormento,
o al menos en su amor contento muere.

Mil penas con un gozo se descuentan,
10   y mil reproches ásperos se vengan
con sólo ver la angélica hermosura.

Mas cuando celos la ánima atormentan,
aunque después mil bienes sobrevengan,
se tornan rabia, pena y amargura.

SAN JUAN DE LA CRUZ
(1542–1591)

JUAN DE YEPES was born at Fontiveros, near Ávila. As a young man he attended the Jesuit college at Medina del Campo and entered the Carmelite order in 1563. From 1564–7, he studied Arts at the University of Salamanca; in 1567 he met Santa Teresa de Jesús for the first time and joined in her plans for a reform of the Carmelite order. After a year's course in theology at Salamanca (1567–8), he took the vows of the Reform and in 1571 became Rector of the College of Discalced Carmelites at Alcalá; a year later he went to Ávila, where he remained until 1577 as confessor to the College of the Incarnation. During these years he was twice kidnapped and imprisoned by opponents of the Reform, the second time in Toledo (1577–8), where he wrote several of his finest poems, including *Aunque es de noche* and part of the *Cántico espiritual*. After escaping from prison in 1578, he became Vicar of El Calvario, in Andalusia, and the next year founded a college of the Reform at Baeza, where he remained as Rector until 1582, when he became Prior of the Granada house of Los Mártires. In the next few years he set up five new foundations in Andalusia, and was for some time Vicar of the province. He left Granada to become Prior of Segovia in 1588; three years later, a few months before his death, he was deprived of his offices by the Madrid Chapter-General, which wrongly suspected him of opposing the current policy of the Reform. He was canonized in 1726.

With Santa Teresa de Jesús, San Juan de la Cruz is one of the two greatest Spanish mystics, and his small body of verse contains several of the finest poems in the language. Scholars have spent much energy on the question of possible sources: there are links with both the Italianate and the popular traditions, and also with contemporary Carmelite verse, which had independently established the *lira* as its chief form of expression. Much has also been made of San Juan's debt to Boscán and Garcilaso, and more particularly to the *a lo divino* version of their poems published by Sebastián de Córdoba in 1575, but apart from the imitation of a passage from Garcilaso's Second Eclogue in the *Cántico espiritual*, the evidence is not convincing. It is clear that San Juan never regarded the writing of poetry as a self-sufficient activity; apart from questions of form, his only true sources are the Bible and his own mystical experience. A much more crucial problem is that of the relation between the three major poems and the extensive prose commentaries on them contained in *La subida del monte Carmelo* (1578–83), *La noche oscura* (begun 1579 and never completed), *Llama de amor viva* (1584) and the *Cántico espiritual* (1584). The basic method of these commentaries, which in themselves are theological texts of unique value, is an impressive demonstration of San Juan's training in the traditional allegorical approach to Scripture. Unless the poems are read in a certain way, he claims, "antes parecen dislates que dichos puestos en razón"; on the other hand, one should be on one's guard against taking the exposition as a substitute for the poems. Often, San Juan's explanation confirms a particular reading or enhances the meaning of a symbol; at other times, it adds a weight of allegorical interpretation for which there is no obvious basis in the poem. The fact is that the commentaries say both less and more than the poems, as San Juan himself seems to suggest in a remark on Biblical commentators: "lo que de ello se declara, ordinariamente es lo menos que contiene en sí". The poems, despite their splendid unity and their brilliant symbols, are only part of an attempt to convey the mystical experience; the commentaries use a different, though often complementary, approach, concerned more directly with the relations between the symbol and the symbolized. *Obras*, ed. P. Silverio de Santa Teresa, 5 vols., Burgos, 1929.

86

CÁNTICO ESPIRITUAL
CANCIONES ENTRE EL ALMA Y EL ESPOSO

ESPOSA

¿Adónde te escondiste,
amado, y me dejaste con gemido?
Como el ciervo huiste,
habiéndome herido;
salí tras ti, clamando, y eras ido.
    Pastores, los que fuerdes
allá, por las majadas, al otero,
si por ventura vierdes
aquel que yo más quiero,
10   decidle que adolezco, peno y muero.
    Buscando mis amores,
iré por esos montes y riberas;
ni cogeré las flores,
ni temeré las fieras,
y pasaré los fuertes y fronteras.

PREGUNTA A LAS CRIATURAS

¡Oh bosques y espesuras,
plantadas por la mano del amado!
¡Oh prado de verduras,
de flores esmaltado,
20   decid si por vosotros ha pasado!

RESPUESTA DE LAS CRIATURAS

Mil gracias derramando,
pasó por estos sotos con presura,
y yéndolos mirando,
con sola su figura
vestidos los dejó de hermosura.

ESPOSA

¡Ay, quién podrá sanarme!
Acaba de entregarte ya de vero;
no quieras enviarme
de hoy más ya mensajero,
30 que no saben decirme lo que quiero.
Y todos cuantos vagan,
de ti me van mil gracias refiriendo,
y todos más me llagan,
y déjame muriendo
un no sé qué que quedan balbuciendo.
Mas ¿cómo perseveras,
oh vida, no viviendo donde vives,
y haciendo porque mueras,
las flechas que recibes,
40 de lo que del amado en ti concibes?
¿Por qué, pues has llagado
aqueste corazón, no le sanaste?
Y pues me le has robado,
¿por qué así le dejaste,
y no tomas el robo que robaste?
Apaga mis enojos,
pues que ninguno basta a deshacellos,
y véante mis ojos,
pues eres lumbre dellos,
50 y sólo para ti quiero tenellos.
Descubre tu presencia,
y máteme tu vista y hermosura;
mira que la dolencia
de amor, que no se cura
sino con la presencia y la figura.
¡Oh cristalina fuente,
si en esos tus semblantes plateados,
formases de repente

los ojos deseados,
60   que tengo en mis entrañas dibujados!
Apártalos, amado,
que voy de vuelo.

EL ESPOSO

Vuélvete, paloma,
que el ciervo vulnerado,
por el otero asoma,
al aire de tu vuelo, y fresco toma.

LA ESPOSA

Mi amado, las montañas,
los valles solitarios nemorosos,
las ínsulas·extrañas,
los ríos sonorosos,
70   el silbo de los aires amorosos,
la noche sosegada,
en par de los levantes de la aurora,
la música callada,
la soledad sonora,
la cena que recrea y enamora.
Nuestro lecho florido,
de cuevas de leones enlazado,
en púrpura tendido,
de paz edificado,
80   de mil escudos de oro coronado.
A zaga de tu huella,
las jóvenes discurren al camino,
al toque de centella,
al adobado vino,
emisiones de bálsamo divino.
En la interior bodega

de mi amado bebí, y cuando salía,
por toda aquesta vega,
ya cosa no sabía,
90   y el ganado perdí que antes seguía.
     Allí me dio su pecho,
allí me enseñó ciencia muy sabrosa,
y yo le di de hecho
a mí, sin dejar cosa,
allí le prometí de ser su esposa.
     Mi alma se ha empleado,
y todo mi caudal, en su servicio;
ya no guardo ganado,
ni ya tengo otro oficio,
100   que ya sólo en amar es mi ejercicio.
     Pues ya si en el ejido
de hoy más no fuere vista ni hallada,
diréis que me he perdido;
que andando enamorada,
me hice perdidiza, y fui ganada.
     De flores y esmeraldas,
en las frescas mañanas escogidas,
haremos las guirnaldas,
en tu amor florecidas,
110   y en un cabello mío entretejidas.
     En sólo aquel cabello
que en mi cuello volar consideraste,
mirástele en mi cuello,
y en él preso quedaste,
y en uno de mis ojos te llagaste.
     Cuando tú me mirabas,
tu gracia en mí tus ojos imprimían;
por eso me adamabas,
y en eso merecían
120   los míos adorar lo que en ti vían.
     No quieras despreciarme,
que si color moreno en mí hallaste,

ya bien puedes mirarme,
después que me miraste,
que gracia y hermosura en mí dejaste.
      Cogednos las raposas,
que está ya florecida nuestra viña,
en tanto que de rosas
hacemos una piña,
130 y no parezca nadie en la montiña.
      Deténte, cierzo muerto;
ven, austro, que recuerdas los amores,
aspira por mi huerto,
y corran sus olores,
y pacerá el amado entre las flores.

ESPOSO

      Entrado se ha la esposa
en el ameno huerto deseado,
y a su sabor reposa,
el cuello reclinado
140 sobre los dulces brazos del amado.
      Debajo del manzano,
allí conmigo fuiste desposada,
allí te di la mano,
y fuiste reparada
donde tu madre fuera vïolada.
      A las aves ligeras,
leones, ciervos, gamos saltadores,
montes, valles, riberas,
aguas, aires, ardores
150 y miedos de las noches veladores,
      por las amenas liras,
y canto de serenas os conjuro,
que cesen vuestras iras,
y no toquéis al muro,
porque la esposa duerma más seguro.

ESPOSA

Oh ninfas de Judea,
en tanto que en las flores y rosales
el ámbar perfumea,
morá en los arrabales,
160   y no queráis tocar nuestros umbrales.
    Escóndete, carillo,
y mira con tu haz a las montañas,
y no quieras decillo;
mas mira las compañas
de la que va por ínsulas extrañas.

ESPOSO

La blanca palomica
al arca con el ramo se ha tornado,
y ya la tortolica
al socio deseado
170   en las riberas verdes ha hallado.
    En soledad vivía,
y en soledad ha puesto ya su nido,
y en soledad la guía
a solas su querido,
también en soledad de amor herido.

ESPOSA

Gocémonos, amado,
y vámonos a ver en tu hermosura
al monte o al collado,
do mana el agua pura,
180   entremos más adentro en la espesura.

        Y luego a las subidas
cavernas de la piedra nos iremos,
que están bien escondidas,
y allí nos entraremos,
y el mosto de granadas gustaremos.
        Allí me mostrarías
aquello que mi alma pretendía,
y luego me darías
allí tú, vida mía,
190   aquello que me diste el otro día.
        El aspirar del aire,
el canto de la dulce filomena,
el soto y su donaire,
en la noche serena
con llama que consume y no da pena.
        Que nadie lo miraba,
Aminadab tampoco parecía,
y el cerco sosegaba,
y la caballería
200   a vista de las aguas descendía.

87

LA NOCHE OSCURA

CANCIONES

*De el alma que se goza de haber llegado al alto estado de la perfección, que es la
unión con Dios, por el camino de la negación espiritual*

        En una noche oscura,
con ansias en amores inflamada,
¡oh dichosa ventura!,
salí sin ser notada,
estando ya mi casa sosegada.
        A escuras y segura,
por la secreta escala disfrazada,

¡oh dichosa ventura!,
a escuras y en celada,
10   estando ya mi casa sosegada.
En la noche dichosa,
en secreto, que nadie me veía,
ni yo miraba cosa,
sin otra luz y guía,
sino la que en el corazón ardía.
Aquésta me guiaba
más cierto que la luz del mediodía,
a donde me esperaba
quien yo bien me sabía,
20   en parte donde nadie parecía.
¡Oh noche que guiaste!
¡oh noche amable más que el alborada!,
¡oh noche que juntaste
amado con amada,
amada en el amado transformada!
En mi pecho florido,
que entero para él solo se guardaba,
alií quedó dormido,
y yo le regalaba,
30   y el ventalle de cedros aire daba.
El aire de la almena,
cuando yo sus cabellos esparcía,
con su mano serena
en mi cuello hería,
y todos mis sentidos suspendía.
Quedéme y olvidéme,
el rostro recliné sobre el amado,
cesó todo, y dejéme,
dejando mi cuidado
40   entre las azucenas olvidado.

88

LLAMA DE AMOR VIVA

CANCIONES

Del alma en la íntima comunicación de unión de amor de Dios.

   ¡Oh llama de amor viva,
que tiernamente hieres
de mi alma en el más profundo centro!,
pues ya no eres esquiva,
acaba ya si quieres,
rompe la tela de este dulce encuentro.
   ¡Oh cauterio süave!,
¡oh regalada llaga!,
¡oh mano blanda!, ¡oh toque delicado,
10   que a vida eterna sabe,
y toda deuda paga!
Matando, muerte en vida la has trocado.
¡Oh lámparas de fuego,
en cuyos resplandores,
las profundas cavernas del sentido,
que estaba oscuro y ciego,
con extraños primores
calor y luz dan junto a su querido!
   ¡Cuán manso y amoroso
20   recuerdas en mi seno,
donde secretamente solo moras:
y en tu aspirar sabroso,
de bien y gloria lleno,
cuán delicadamente me enamoras!

89

AUNQUE ES DE NOCHE

CANTAR DE LA ALMA QUE SE HUELGA DE
CONOCER A DIOS POR FE

Que bien sé yo la fonte que mana y corre,
    aunque es de noche.
Aquella eterna fonte está ascondida,
que bien sé yo do tiene su manida,
    aunque es de noche.
Su origen no lo sé, pues no le tiene,
mas sé que todo origen della viene,
    aunque es de noche.
Sé que no puede ser cosa tan bella,
10 y que cielos y tierra beben de ella,
    aunque es de noche.
Bien sé que suelo en ella no se halla,
y que ninguno puede vadealla,
    aunque es de noche.
Su claridad nunca es escurecida,
y sé que toda luz de ella es venida,
    aunque es de noche.
Sé ser tan caudalosos sus corrientes,
que infiernos, cielos riegan, y las gentes,
20   aunque es de noche.
El corriente que nace de esta fuente,
bien sé que es tan capaz y omnipotente,
    aunque es de noche.
El corriente que de estas dos procede
sé que ninguna de ellas le precede,
    aunque es de noche.
Aquesta eterna fonte está escondida
en este vivo pan por darnos vida,
    aunque es de noche.

30   Aquí se está llamando a las criaturas,
y de esta agua se hartan, aunque a escuras
porque es de noche.
Aquesta viva fuente, que deseo,
en este pan de vida yo la veo,
aunque de noche.

90

TRAS DE UN AMOROSO LANCE

Tras de un amoroso lance,
y no de esperanza falto,
volé tan alto, tan alto,
que le di a la caza alcance.
Para que yo alcance diese
a aqueste lance divino,
tanto volar me convino,
que de vista me perdiese;
y con todo, en este trance,
10   en el vuelo quedé falto;
mas el amor fue tan alto,
que le di a la caza alcance.
Cuando más alto subía,
deslumbróseme la vista,
y la más fuerte conquista
en escuro se hacía;
mas por ser de amor el lance
di un ciego y oscuro salto,
y fui tan alto, tan alto,
20   que le di a la caza alcance.
Cuanto más alto llegaba
de este lance tan subido,
tanto más bajo y rendido
y abatido me hallaba.
Dije: ¡No habrá quien alcance!

Y abatíme tanto, tanto,
que fui tan alto, tan alto,
que le di a la caza alcance.
　　Por una extraña manera
30　mil vuelos pasé de un vuelo,
porque esperanza de cielo
tanto alcanza cuanto espera;
esperé sólo este lance,
y en esperar no fui falto,
pues fui tan alto, tan alto,
que le di a la caza alcance.

91

EL PASTORCICO

CANCIONES A LO DIVINO, DE CRISTO Y EL ALMA

　　Un pastorcico solo está penado,
ajeno de placer y de contento,
y en su pastora puesto el pensamiento,
y el pecho del amor muy lastimado.
　　No llora por haberle amor llagado,
que no le pena verse así afligido,
aunque en el corazón está herido;
mas llora por pensar que está olvidado.
　　Que sólo de pensar que está olvidado
10　de su bella pastora, con gran pena,
se deja maltratar en tierra ajena,
el pecho del amor muy lastimado.
　　Y dice el pastorcico: ¡Ay desdichado
de aquel que de mi amor ha hecho ausencia,
y no quiere gozar la mi presencia,
y el pecho por su amor muy lastimado!
　　Y a cabo de un gran rato se ha encumbrado
sobre un árbol, do abrió sus brazos bellos,
y muerto se ha quedado, asido de ellos,
20　el pecho del amor muy lastimado.

NOTES TO THE POEMS

La mucha tristeza mía (p. 1)

2. *vuestro deseo*: "my desire for you".

39–40. *que a mí . . . la tristeza de él*: "it was not love which killed me, but the sadness which comes (came) from love".

67. *el ausencia*: As late as the seventeenth century, *el* was used instead of *la* before a feminine singular noun beginning with a vowel, particularly *a*, whether stressed or not.

79. *recordé*: "desperté".

Secáronme los pesares (p. 4)

3. *que no pueden llorar, non*: This repetition of *no(n)* at the end of a phrase is a common device in traditional poetry. Cf. *Romance de Fontefrida*: "que no quiero ser tu amiga / ni casar contigo, no!".

23. *tanta tengo de razón*: "I have so much reason to feel sorrowful that I cannot weep".

En el placiente verano (p. 5)

The use of a single full rhyme instead of assonance in the even-numbered lines is characteristic of late fifteenth-century *romances*. (See Introduction, p. xiii.)

Madre, cuando enviudaré (p. 6)

9. *bien sabidas*: in the sense that everyone knows their history, as the speaker herself claims in the next line.

Ojos garzos ha la niña (p. 11)

6. *ell alegría*: "el (la) alegría". (See note to "La mucha tristeza mía", l. 67, above.)

No te tardes que me muero (p. 12)

19. *la primer vez*: *primero* was occasionally apocopated before a feminine noun in the sixteenth century.

25. *galardonarme*: in the terminology of courtly love, the *galardón* is the reward, spiritual or physical, which the lady grants her lover in return for his faithfulness.

Por unos puertos arriba (p. 13)

22. *asegura:* "está seguro".

31–3. The final *estribillo* was glossed several times by Encina, once in an *a lo divino* version: "—¿Quién te trajo, Criador, / por esta montaña escura? / —¡Ay que tú, mi criatura!". It was also used by Alvarez Gato and, later, by Santa Teresa. For the rhyme-scheme of the *romance,* see Introduction, p. xiii.

En la huerta nace la rosa (p. 16)

In this poem and others, Gil Vicente uses a technique of repetition *(paralelismo)* derived from the Galician-Portuguese *cantares de amigo.* (See Note on Versification, under *canción paralelística.)*

Halcón que se atreve (p. 16)

For other poems which use hawking imagery, see Cetina, "Como garza real, alta en el cielo" (p. 70) and San Juan de la Cruz, "Tras de un amoroso lance" (p. 144).

Vanse mis amores, madre (p. 18)

2. *luengas tierras van morar:* "van a morar en tierras lejanas".

No pueden dormir mis ojos (p. 23)

1–2. The *estribillo* is taken from an older poem which appears in the *Cancionero musical de los siglos XV y XVI* ed. by F. Asenjo Barbieri, Madrid, 1890.

Hola, gentil Galatea (p. 23)

The source of the poem is Ovid, *Metamorphoses,* Book XIII. Polyphemus, the Cyclops, was one of the children of Neptune (see l. 333); his love for the sea-nymph Galatea, and his jealousy of his rival, the shepherd Acis, gave Renaissance poets a unique opportunity for combining the mythological fable with the pastoral.

90. *tela:* "se toma asimismo por el sitio cerrado y dispuesto para fiestas, lides públicas y otros espectáculos" *(Diccionario de autoridades,* 1726).

Ahí van las ansias mías (p. 37)

3. *pintadas:* in the sense of "feigned".

19. *figuras:* "images, foreshadowings". These lines are strikingly similar to a passage in John Donne's poem *The Good-Morrow:* "If ever any beauty I did see, / which I desir'd, and got, 'twas but a dream of thee".

Como aquel que en soñar gusto recibe (p. 39)

This poem is an imitation of Ausias March, I, ll. 1–8: "Així com cell qui en lo somni es delita . . .". In this poem and the next, Boscán reproduces a type of extended comparison which is very characteristic of Ausias March and was to become an unmistakeable hallmark of his influence among Castilian poets of the period.

3. *figura*: "feigning".

Como el patrón que, en golfo navegando (p. 39)

The first four lines of this poem are based on Ausias March, II, ll. 1–8: "Pren-me enaixí com al patró que en platja . . .", but the rest, including the fine last tercet, is original.

1. *patrón*: here, the master of a ship.

10. *acude'l*: "acúdele, le acude". The apostrophe is necessary for the scansion.

¡ Quién viese aquel día (p. 40)

4. *bando*: "strife".

Escrito está en mi alma vuestro gesto (p. 43)

1. Cf. Petrarch, Sonnet V, l. 14: "E'l nome che nel cor mi scrisse Amore", and Ausias March, LXII, l. 49: "Ma opinió és en mon cor escrita".

4. *tan solo*: "tan secretamente".

7–8. *de tanto bien . . . por presupuesto*: This kind of pseudo-religious argument is common in Ausias March and Boscán. The idea of love as a religion is one of the basic themes of *cancionero* poetry.

9. *Yo no nací sino para quereros*: Cf. Ausias March, LVIII, l. 30: "Per vos amar fou lo meu naixement".

10–11. The clothes metaphor also appears in Sonnet XXVII: "Amor, amor, un hábito vestí, / el cual de vuestro paño fue cortado", where it is taken directly from Ausias March, LXXVII, l. 25: "Amor, Amor, un hàbit m'he tallat / de vostre drap . . .".

A Dafne ya los brazos le crecían (p. 44)

Daphne was transformed into a laurel-bush to escape from Apollo, whose tears watered the plant and kept it green. In Garcilaso's poem, the visual rendering of the transformation is particularly fine; notice the immediacy of *vi* (l. 3) and the vivid use of *bullendo* (l. 6) to suggest the movement of the limbs.

En tanto que de rosa y azucena (p. 44)

The structure of this poem resembles that of Bernardo Tasso's sonnet "Mentre che l'aureo crin ondeggia in torno", but there are also reminisences of the two great classical versions of the theme, Horace's ode to Ligurinus (Book IV, x) and the "Collige, virgo, rosas" of Ausonius. Many Renaissance poets, beginning with Lorenzo de' Medici (1449–1492) attempted the *carpe diem* theme; Garcilaso's treatment has great dignity and a quiet elegance which is very effective.

4. In the earliest editions this line reads: "con clara luz la tempestad serena". Herrera gives the present reading on the authority of Garcilaso's son-in-law, Antonio Puertocarrero.

Con un manso rüido (p. 45)

For the circumstances of this poem, see biographical note, p. 42.

26. *por sólo aquello*: "solamente porque espero morir".

31. *que mal librado quede*: "que acabe mal".

32. *otra prenda*: i.e. the spirit.

37–8. *que otra cosa . . . ha hallado*: i.e. the pain caused by love. This type of word-play *(hallar . . . me hallas . . . ha hallado)* is a common feature of *cancionero* poetry.

Aquella voluntad honesta y pura (p. 47)

2. *ilustre y hermosísima María*: In addressing these courtly compliments to a great lady—possibly the wife of the Viceroy of Naples, Don Pedro de Toledo—Garcilaso consciously comes to terms with the pastoral convention, notably in the ambiguous modesty of ll. 41–8. The verve with which he expands a Virgilian reminiscence in l. 11 *(Georgics*, IV, l. 525: "vox ipsa et frigida lingua") is typical of the whole passage.

29. *las hermanas, todas nueve*: the Muses.

55–6. *Filódoce . . . no tiene*: the names of the nymphs are taken from Book XVIII of the *Iliad* and Book IV of the *Georgics*.

57 etc. This passage (ll. 57–96) and a later one (ll. 201–32) are brilliantly analysed by Dámaso Alonso in *Poesía española*, pp. 45–109 (see Bibliography). In both passages, the metre, rhythm and syntax play an important part in establishing the atmosphere of the description.

61. *y así la teje arriba y encadena*: The suggestion is that Nature herself is an artist, creating both the shady grove and the music of the river.

70–1. *una ninfa . . . la cabeza sacó*: Notice the vivid placing of *sacó*; the abruptness of the hiatus is accentuated by the *enjambement* immediately before it.

84. *y al fondo se dejó calar del río*: The dislocation of normal word-order (hyperbaton) prolongs the visual effect of the action.

89 etc. There are precedents for the tapestry episode in Virgil *(Georgics*, Book IV) and Sannazaro *(Arcadia*, Prosa XII).

94. *nadando dividieron y cortaron*: Cf. Dámaso Alonso: "El nadador . . . separa *(divide)* el agua con los brazos; la *corta* con el cuerpo, que avanza como una saeta" (op. cit., p. 83).

110. *estambre sutil*: i.e. silk. Garcilaso is emphasizing the process by which the raw materials of Nature (gold-dust, leaves, natural dyes) become the materials of art. There is an analogy between the work of the nymphs and that of the poet: words such as *convenía* and *estilo* suggest Renaissance theories of poetic decorum.

120. *el celebrado Apeles y Timantes*: two ancient Greek painters, both famous for their skill in creating pictures which gave the illusion of real life.

124. *Estrimón*: the Strymon, the river in Thrace which is the setting of the Orpheus myth.

128. *del de Tracia*: Orpheus, who was allowed to bring Eurydice back to earth on condition that he did not look at her while they were travelling through the infernal regions. The "tyrant" (l. 143) is Pluto, Lord of Hades.

147 etc. See the note to "A Dafne ya los brazos le crecían" (p. 149), an earlier treatment of the same theme.

160. *el odioso plomo*: Cupid traditionally has two kinds of arrow: those of gold bring irresistible love, those of lead cause everlasting revulsion.

178. *aquel mancebo*: Adonis, Venus's lover, killed in jealousy by the god Mars, who changed himself into a wild boar.

193 etc. *La blanca Nise*: The subject of the fourth tapestry is not a classical myth, but the death of Elisa (Isabel Freire), already mourned by Nemoroso in the First Eclogue. But by presenting his private experience in this way, Garcilaso is deliberately creating a new myth, in which personal grief is transformed into an objective work of art. This process is emphasized by the description of the Tagus flowing past Toledo: the river is no longer merely part of the idealized setting; it is the real river on which Garcilaso's native city stands.

216. *con artificio de las altas ruedas*: the irrigation-wheels *(azudes)* by which water was raised from the river to the city. The use of the word *artificio* suggests that this is another example of nature in the service of art.

230. *degollada*: Cf. Herrera, *Anotaciones*: "Dice *degollada* por *desangrada*".

231–2. *el blanco cisne*: The image of the dying swan, by suggesting that death may give rise to song, is central to the purpose of the poem.

268. *claras las luces, de las sombras vanas*: *Vanas* here means "illusory": "las cuales (telas), con colores matizadas, mostraban a los ojos las cosas y figuras . .
claras las luces (ablative absolute) relevadas de las sombras vanas". The passage resembles descriptions of *chiaroscuro* in Renaissance manuals on painting: the figures are given relief *(relevadas)* by making the highlights *(claras luces)* appear to stand out from the shadows.

289 etc. The conclusion of the poem gradually moves away from the theme of personal sorrow. The technical description of the tapestries (ll. 265–72) is followed by a return to the idyllic atmosphere of the opening stanzas (ll. 273–88). Finally, the pastoral songs of Tirreno and Alcino, with their conventional allusions to rustic happiness and fertility, mark the poet's return to a world which will not remind him of the past and in which new experiences are still possible.

353. *Alcides*: Hercules.

Tu gracia, tu valor, tu hermosura (p. 62)

7. *retraerte*: " retratarte". The woman's beauty, since it is divine, cannot be directly observed. But in the lover's soul it is reduced *(abreviada)* to human form, and it is this form which the artist has painted.

Cual simple mariposa vuelvo al fuego (p. 62)

Basically an imitation of Petrarch, *Rime* CXLI ("Come talora al caldo tempo sòle . . ."), though Mendoza emphasizes the power of the woman's beauty, rather than her disdain. (Cf. Herrera's sonnet on the same theme, p. 101.)

Señor Gómez Arias (p. 63)

The origin of the legend of Gómez Arias, who seduces a Christian girl and later sells her to a Moor, is unknown. No ballad version has survived, though the four lines glossed by Horozco were well-known in the sixteenth and seventeenth centuries and the story was used in *comedias* by Vélez de Guevara and Calderón. The phrase *mal entendida* probably refers to the existence of burlesque references like that in *La lozana andaluza* (1528). (See also Note on Versification, under *zéjel.)*

Un novillo feroz y un fuerte toro (p. 67)

The theme, but little else, is taken from a sonnet by Lodovico Domenichi (d. 1564), "Al cozzar di due tauri arditi e forti". The force of Acuña's poem comes from the juxtaposition of the two contrasting groups—the rival bulls and the chorus of nymphs—and the way in which both are worked into the lovers' situation. Notice the effect of *vi* in l. 6—a device perhaps copied from Garcilaso's sonnet on Daphne and Apollo (see note on p. 149).

Ojos claros, serenos (p. 69)

Cetina's poem bears a striking resemblance to a *villancico* published in the *Romancero general* (1600): "Aunque, con semblante airado / me miráis, ojos serenos, / no me negaréis, al menos, / ojos, que me habéis mirado". It is not known which poem was the source of the other; in either case, the link with the *cancionero* tradition is clear.

Por vos ardí, señora, y por vos ardo (p. 70)

An imitation of Tansillo's sonnet LXVII, "Io arsi per voi, donna, e per voi ardo". The image in l. 14 reappears in one of Quevedo's finest sonnets, "Cerrar podrá mis ojos la postrera / sombra . . .": "nadar sabe mi llama la agua fría".

Como garza real, alta en el cielo (p. 70)

For other poems which use hawking imagery, see Gil Vicente, "Halcón que se atreve" (p. 16) and San Juan de la Cruz, "Tras de un amoroso lance" (p. 144).

7. *él:* This refers to *desconsuelo* in the following line. The sense of the whole quatrain is: "realizing by the hidden power of instinct that death awaits her

on the ground, no sooner is she seized by despair ("del desconsuelo aque-
jada') than she gives voice to it".

11. *para me levantar remontadores*: His previous loves were like the birds used to
"put up" the game. It is the present one which kills, like the falcon which
is held in check until the others have tired the quarry.

Decid, los que tratáis de agricultura (p. 72)

8. *silo*: "Lugar subterráneo y enjuto, a donde se guarda el trigo" (Covar-
rubias, *Tesoro de la lengua castellana*, 1611).

13. *baratar*: here, "ganar", "sacar".

La vida se nos pasa, el tiempo vuela (p. 73)

3. *Atropos*: Of the three Fates *(Parcas)*, it is Atropos who cuts the thread of
life.

4. *la Muerte hace mangas desta tela*: Perhaps there is also a suggestion of the
figurative meaning contained in the phrase "hacer mangas y capirotes": "to
do something quickly, without thought".

5. *la cargada navezuela*: the ship of life.

8. *consúmese el humor, muere la vela*: Both the body's fluid and the wax of the
candle *(vela)* are used up. In the first part of the metaphor, it is the action
of breathing which causes the wick (of life) to burn.

Mortales: ¿habéis visto mayor cosa (p. 73)

This sonnet is spoken by Death.

Soy garridica (p. 75)

1. *garridica*: diminutive of "garrida".

Tres serranas he encontrado (p. 76)

12. *monjiles*: here, "open sleeves".

17. *antiparas*: leggings worn by reapers.

¡ Sea bienvenida, sea (p. 80)

This is a *canción de bienvenida a lo divino*. For a secular example, see Lope de Vega,
Fuenteovejuna, I, vi: "Sea bienvenido, / el Comendadore".

De dentro tengo mi mal (p. 81)

This poem is a gloss *(volta)* on a two-line theme *(mote)* from another poet.

Irme quiero, madre (p. 82)

The seafaring imagery of this poem reflects the *barcarolas* of the Galician-Portuguese tradition.

9. *Aquel niño fiero:* Cupid.

El vaso reluciente y cristalino (p. 83)

9. *Nel vaso vuestro corpo:* "En el vaso vuestro cuerpo"; *se figura:* "The vase (in the metaphor) stands for your body". The key to the different parts of the comparison is in the tercets, but the strength and delicate effect of the poem come from the quatrains, in which the terms of the basic metaphor (body-glass) are not yet clearly separated.

¡ Qué descansada vida (p. 86)

3–4. *la escondida / senda:* This has a triple meaning: (i) literally, the road leading to La Flecha, the Augustinian retreat outside Salamanca which is the setting for the dialogue in *De los nombres de Cristo;* (ii) the hidden path by which the soul escapes from worldly vanity; (iii) Christ himself ("I am the Way . . .").

11. *No cura:* "no se preocupa".

19. *desalentado:* "discouraged", but also "out of breath". The pun is based on the meaning of *viento* in the previous line: "the wind of (hollow) fame", which leads only to death *(mortal cuidado).*

36. *Vivir quiero conmigo:* Cf. *Nombres, Príncipe de Paz:* "Porque el que tiene consigo guerra, no es posible que en ninguna cosa halle contento puro y sencillo".

39. *libre de amor, de celo:* These are the *cuidados graves* (l. 33) which pursue the man of power: love and zeal based on earthly values, and therefore false.

41 etc. *Del monte en la ladera:* The *huerto* is both literal and symbolic: *por mi mano plantado* suggests that the spiritual fruit *(cierto fruto,* as only divine fruit can be) must be planted by the will of the tenant. The "greed" of the stream *(fontana . . . codiciosa)* is beneficent, unlike that of the man of power; in the rest of the allegory, the waters (of the spirit) flow down from the hill (Christ) to refresh the trees (the souls of men). These symbolic meanings are elaborated in various passages of the *Nombres,* where both *Camino* and *Monte* are synonyms of Christ.

70. *y la mar enriquecen a porfía:* The merchants are throwing their goods into the sea to lighten the ship: *a porfía:* "vying with one another".

76–7. *miserable- / mente:* The *enjambement* emphasizes the sense of these lines, whose broken rhythm contrasts with the smooth repetition—*tendido yo . . . A la sombra tendido*—which reintroduces the theme of spiritual harmony.

82. *de hiedra y lauro eterno coronado:* The trappings of earthly power (the *no durable mando* of l. 79) are now the symbols of moral and spiritual strength.

El aire se serena (p. 89)

Francisco de Salinas (1514–1590) was Professor of Music at the University of

Salamanca; though blind from birth, he was a fine organist and the author of a treatise on musical theory, *De Musica* (1577). Several of the basic concepts of the poem appear in similar form in the writings of St. Augustine.

6–10. The idea that the human soul forgets its heavenly origin is a commonplace of pre-Socratic philosophy. Cf. Wordsworth, *Immortality Ode*: "Our birth is but a sleep and a forgetting".

11. *Y como se conoce*: As it comes to understand its divine nature, the soul achieves its true *suerte*, the love of God.

16 etc. *traspasa el aire todo*: In the Ptolemaic system of astronomy, the earth is at the centre of the universe; only in the highest sphere, the Empyrean, can things be seen in their true nature.

21–5. *Ve cómo el gran maestro*: This stanza is missing in some manuscripts, but there can be no doubt of its authenticity. Aristotle, basing himself on Pythagorean doctrine, explains that each sphere as it moves emits a different musical note; these notes harmonize with one another to produce the "music of the spheres". In Luis de León's image, the universe is a lyre in the hands of God the musician. St. Augustine (Letter 138, para. 5) speaks of the beauty of the temporal world as "the great song of an ineffable musician" ("magnum carmen . . . ineffabilis modulatoris").

26–35. *Y como está compuesta . . . o siente*: The subject is *mi alma* (1. 7). The human will and the Will of God blend in a musical counterpoint in which the sense of human identity is lost *(se anega)*. This oblivion is very different from the *olvido* of l. 7. *Accidente* refers to the contingencies of earthly life.

43. *amigos*: Mayans, in his edition of 1761, suggests the singular *amigo* as more appropriate to the context. The scansion, however, requires the plural.

Cuando contemplo el cielo (p. 90)

6–10. Notice the skilful gradation *(pecho . . . ojos . . . lengua)* which leads into the invocation.

15. *en esta cárcel baja escura*: This has been taken to refer to the poet's imprisonment. It seems more likely that he is using the Platonic metaphor of the world as the soul's prison. Cf. "Alma región luciente", l. 38, below.

16. *desatino*: here, "error".

24. *vueltas dando*: in Ptolemaic astronomy, the sky moves round the stationary earth.

37. *el bajo y torpe suelo*: Montaigne *(Essais, II, xii)* calls the earth "la pire, plus morte et croupie partie de l'univers, (le) dernier étage du logis et le plus éloigné de la voûte céleste".

38. *trasunto*: In Platonic theory, heaven contains the archetypes or ideal forms of all earthly things.

44. *sus pasos desiguales*: the separate orbits of the spheres.

46–60. The spheres appear in the order allotted to them in the Ptolemaic system, with the omission of the sun: the moon, Mercury *(la luz do el saber llueve)*, Venus, Mars, Jupiter and Saturn, the father of the "golden ages" of prosperity. After the seventh heaven *(la cumbre)* come the stars *(la muche-dumbre del reluciente coro)* and the Empyrean, which, as here (ll. 66–80), was often equated with the Christian heaven.

Alma región luciente (p. 93)

Much of the Biblical imagery on which this poem is based is expanded, often with striking similarities of phrasing, in the *Pastor* section of *De los nombres de Cristo*.

4. *fallece*: the subject is *prado*, not *región*.

6–7. *De púrpura . . . coronado*: "la cabeza coronada de flores purpúreas y blancas" *La cabeza coronado . . .* is an example of the Greek accusative construction ("crowned as to the head"), used in classical Latin and occasionally imitated by Spanish writers in the sixteenth and seventeenth centuries. Cf. Garcilaso, *Égloga segunda*, l. 144: "las venas dulcemente desatado".

9. *sin honda ni cayado*: i.e. unlike a human shepherd.

10. *en ti*: refers back to *región* (l. 1).

18. *fiel*: "del alma que ha sido fiel a Dios".

20. *pastor y pasto él solo*: as in the Eucharist.

21–3. *Y de su esfera . . . el sol*: "Y cuando el sol . . . toca la cumbre de su esfera".

28. *envilece*: here, "desprecia, tiene por vil".

30. *libre de tasa*: "'freely-given'".

40. *viviré junta, sin vagar errada*: There are a number of variants of this line, none of them completely satisfactory. I have followed the Quevedo text, in which the shift of tense changes the emphasis from aspiration *(conocería)* to resolution *(viviré)*. On this reading, the feminine forms *(desatada . . . junta . . . errada)* would be justified by the relationship between Christ and the human soul implied in l. 37 *(dulce Esposo)*. In the final stanza, the soul ("la Esposa") is speaking in the first person (cf. San Juan de la Cruz, *Cántico espiritual*). P. Llobera, S.J., in his edition of 1931, replaces *viviré* by *viviera*, which makes *alma* (l. 34) the subject of the verbs in the final stanza. This makes for stricter syntax, but goes against the effect of direct speech in the first person created by *mi sentido* and *sesteas*. P. Vega and several other recent editors prefer the Merino text of 1816, which has "junta, no ya andará perdida, errada". There is a manuscript tradition for this reading, although the rhythmical effect is clumsy.

¡ Y dejas, Pastor santo (p. 94)

In all but one manuscript, this poem ends at l. 25. The shorter version is more dramatic, but the additional stanzas are almost certainly authentic, and the whole poem forms a religious meditation of a type recommended in the *Spiritual exercises* of St. Ignatius (1548). Thus, the "composition of place" (the scene of the Ascension) is followed by the "application of the senses", particularly of sight. The additional stanzas explore the meaning in terms of the individual soul, and end with an exhortation to accept death *(la salida)* and a "resolution" to follow Christ in this life and the next.

20. *la nave:* the Church.

22. *¿Qué te aquejas?,* "¿Qué te apuras?, ¿Por qué te das tanta prisa?".

26. *el tesoro:* Christ, who ascended to heaven in a cloud.

39–40. *Sin cuerpo . . . presencia:* After death, the soul must exist apart from the body until the resurrection.

44. *en tenebroso* (lugar): on earth.

Id, suspiros ardientes (p. 96)

The ultimate source of this poem is Petrarch's sonnet "Ite caldi sospiri . . ." (*Rime,* CLIII), but Alcázar may have known the madrigal version which appears in *Madrigali . . . da diversi eccellentissimi autori,* Venice, 1555.

Rasga la venda y mira lo que haces (p. 97)

1. *Rasga la venda:* Cupid is traditionally blindfold.

No bañes en el mar sagrado y cano (p. 99)

6. *Náyades:* Naiads, river nymphs.

7–9. *Aquí . . . de Turca gente:* The allusion to the fleet recently returned from the battle of Lepanto suggests that the episode to which the poem refers took place late in 1571. The association of heroism in a national and religious cause with the theme of love is characteristic of Herrera.

16. *Tú amaste:* The love of the river Betis (Guadalquivir) for the nymph Galatea, based on a reference in the Roman poet Martial, is the theme of a later elegy (1619 ed., I, 8). Cf. also *Rimas inéditas,* Egl. I, ll. 20–4.

25. *perlas:* i.e. "teeth". The use of "ennobling" metaphors for parts of the body is common practice among poets of the Italianate tradition.

26. *teñido:* In the 1582 version, this line reads "teñido el rostro de color de rosa"; though the noun *rostro* has been eliminated in the 1619 text, the agreement *(teñido)* has been retained, to the detriment of the sense.

52–3. *Las . . . penas:* This violent hyperbaton appears only in the 1619 text. The 1582 version reads: "Las penas que por sola vos sostengo / me dan valor . . .".

56. *que vos probéis el daño:* "that you should suffer harm for it".

67–73. The implication is that only by day will the lover receive the favours of his lady (cf. ll. 22–4); night, associated with tears *(húmido semblante),* is a time for regret. Critics eager for biographical clues have read too much into l. 67: the context suggests an unfulfilled promise, like those described in the elegy *Al desengaño* (1619 ed., I, 7): "sombras fueron de bien las que yo tuve; / oscuras sombras en la luz más clara".

Vuela y cerca la lumbre y no reposa (p. 101)

This is a reworking of an earlier sonnet, "La incauta y descuidada mariposa", (*Rimas inéditas,* XXIV, pp. 59–60), which is an imitation of Petrarch, *Rime* CXLI: "Come talora al caldo tempo sòle / semplicetta farfalla . . .". In the later version, Herrera reinterprets the original metaphor by introducing the neo-Platonic image of the soul as a moth which seeks to be united with the flame of beauty. Petrarch's sonnet was imitated by a number of sixteenth-century poets, including Diego Hurtado de Mendoza (see p. 62), Cetina and Camoens.

1–2. Notice the dramatic succession of verbs.

3. *figura simple suya*: *simple* here is carried over from Petrarch's original phrase "semplicetta farfalla", though the noun ("farfalla" = "mariposa") is suppressed. *Figura* suggests both the moth as a literal "image" of the candle flame and the soul as a "figment" of ideal beauty.

8. *cobrarse*: "recobrarse".

Dulce el fuego de Amor, dulce la pena (p. 102)

9. *esta Luz pura de belleza*: *Luz* is the most common of Herrera's pseudonyms for the Condesa de Gelves. (See biographical note.)

Alma, que ya en la luz del puro cielo (p. 102)

This poem, like the last, appears in an earlier version in the 1578 manuscript. It is a literary exercise, written during the lifetime of the Condesa de Gelves, and suggested by Petrarch's poems on the death of Laura.

2–3. *a quien suspira . . . mira*: The sense is "mira con suaves ojos a quien llora tu ausencia".

13. *esta sombra*: the earth.

Ahora que cubrió de blanco hielo (p. 103)

1. *de blanco hielo*: The 1578 version has "velo" for *hielo*. This brings out what is less obvious in the 1619 text, that the woman *(la hermosa Aurora mía)* is wearing white. (Cf. ll. 10–11: *pues tiene en blanca nieve el pecho tierno . . . defendido.*) *Hielo*, on the other hand, immediately strikes the note which is held so effectively through the rest of the poem. The woman's hair *(el oro)* is a symbol of the perfect beauty which is the goal of Platonic love; in covering it in white, she invests all the other attributes of love with the new colour. This leads to a further play on *hielo* in ll. 8 and 14. The fire–ice contrast is a commonplace of Renaissance love poetry. (Cf. l. 14 of the following poem.)

5–6. *viras . . . arco*: the weapon of Cupid.

Rojo sol, que con llama gloriosa (3 versions) (pp. 104–5)

The three versions, taken chronologically, show an increasing emphasis on colour effects and precious materials *(llama gloriosa—hacha luminosa; profundo—purpúreo; dorado velo—el oro . . . y rico velo; formas—lumbres—astros)* and a tendency to eliminate sound-clashes and conventional epithets *(hallaste . . . igualaste—hallaste . . . iguale; mi bella Luz—mi serena Luz; ¿ vistes vos mis penas—vistes mis dolores).* (1582 version)

1. *hacha*: "antorcha".

Voz de dolor y canto de gemido (p. 105)

On 4th August 1578, the young King Sebastian of Portugal and many of the Portuguese nobility died in the Battle of Alcázarquivir, in N.E. Morocco. The expedition, carried out in support of the pretender to the throne of Morocco, Muley Hamet, was rash and insufficiently prepared. Herrera sees the defeat as a divine punishment for greed and temerity, though in a sonnet on the same theme (1619 ed., I, 67), he refers to "los excelsos héroes" and "las no rendidas almas generosas". The whole poem is a skilful tissue of Old Testament allusions, the most important of which are as follows:
l. 1: *Jeremiah* xxxi, 15; l. 14: *Isaiah* xxxi, 1; ll. 24–6: *Isaiah* xxxi, 3, *Exodus* xv, 21; ll. 28–39: *Isaiah* xiii, 9–18; ll. 67–91: *Numbers* xxiv, 6, *Daniel* iv, 10–17.

9. *dende el áfrico Atlante y seno ardiente*: "from the Atlas Mountains and the burning desert to the Red Sea".

30. *de gente y de placer el reino ajeno*: Despite the 1582 and 1619 texts, both of which place a comma after *gente*, the sense is: "puso en soledad . . . y en llanto el reino ajeno de ('bereft of') gente y de placer".

34. *visitó sobre*: This phrase, which appears strained in Castilian, is an over-literal translation of the Vulgate: "Et visitabo super orbis mala . . ." (*Isaiah* xiii, 11).

37. *que*: "para que".

57. *las hórridas naciones*: "the barbarous nations". The allusion is to Portuguese colonization in the East.

65. *justamente*: "with due rites".

85. *por la raíz cortado*: The short line, and the pause which follows it, dramatically underline the sense at this point.

92. *Libia*: here, Morocco.

103. *Luco*: the river which runs close to Alcázarquivir.

Mil veces callo que romper deseo (p. 112)

8. *casi en sombra de muerte un nuevo Orfeo*: "like a second Orpheus among the shades of death" (see note on p. 151). *Casi* = "como", like Italian "quasi".

En fin, en fin, tras tanto andar muriendo (p. 112)

11. *dél*: "de él". i.e. "del mundo".

Montano, cuyo nombre es la primera (p. 113)

1. *Montano*: Benito Arias Montano (1527–1598), the great Biblical scholar and friend of Luis de León. Cf. Rivers, ed. cit., p. xxiv: "Aldana . . . pertenecía al mismo grupo de pensadores religiosos, los que pueden ser considerados descendientes neo-platónicos de los erasmistas".

1–2. *la primera / estrellada señal*: a submerged pun on the name "Arias" and "Aries", the sign of the Zodiac which the sun (*Apolo*, l. 4) enters at the beginning of spring.

9. *Eolo*: Aeolus, the god of the winds.

28. *interese*: "interés". Aldana is probably thinking of his personal difficulties in the Netherlands under the governorship of Requesens, who replaced the Duque de Alba in 1573.

34. *cuatro veces ciento* etc.: *El planeta septeno* is the moon; 480 revolutions = 40 years, Aldana's age at the time of writing.

39. *crüel, doblado tiro*: The "double injury" connects with *dos infiernos* (l. 15) and *doble trato* (l. 45).

48. *jornada de*: "camino de".

50. *y platicar en él mi interior hombre*: *platicar* = "practicar, tratar". Cf. St. Paul, *Romans* vii, 22: "For I delight in the law of God after the inward man".

56. *Eco*: the nymph Echo in the legend of Narcissus. (Cf. 1. 63.) Echo hiding in a cave is like the soul imprisoned in the body, from whose depths it nevertheless echoes the divine lover.

68. *ella no encuentra*: The subject is *alma* (l. 59); modern Spanish would demand a reflexive: "se encuentra".

70. *desencentra*: "quita de su centro". The metaphor is taken from the process of scent-making.

73. *destilará*: The subject is *alma*, to which *la* (l. 75) also refers.

85. *cual pece dentro el vaso alto, estupendo*: *pece* = "pez"; *estupendo* = "maravilloso".

93. *sin que lugar adquiere peregrino*: "without moving from its usual place", in contrast to the *lugar que sobre el mundo alcanza*, i.e. which awaits it in heaven *En él* (l. 98) refers back to *el lugar*.

99. *casi el velo mortal sin animarse*: ("estando) el velo mortal, el cuerpo, casi sin vida", since the soul has almost abandoned it.

104. *cual gota de licor que el rostro enciende*: "cual gota de sudor". The individual soul is still part of creation, even when it is reunited with its Creator.

140. *aquel sin hacer pie luengo vacío*: "aquel gran vacío donde no se puede hacer pie".

150. *sálgase a ver del tiempo en la corriente*: "salga a verse en la corriente del tiempo".

151. *producida*: "produced" in the geometrical sense.

165. *del Impíreo*: The Empyrean, in Ptolemaic astronomy, the region beyond the stars, commonly identified with the Christian heaven.

168. *ni hay tal naturaleza*: "porque su naturaleza no les permite hacer esto".

191. *toda del suelo alta abertura*: "toda la alta abertura del suelo".

210. *de nuestra indignidad que no le arguya*: "para que no le acuse (al ser humano) de nuestra indignidad, de nuestra falta de merecimientos".

217. *que allí la diligencia menos halla*: Aldana is arguing that if one deliberately attempts to seek grace, one is likely to end in spiritual conflict.

225. *humor*: "líquido".

237. *no le pidiendo*: "si no se lo pide".

238-9. *verá . . . regarse*: "se verá regar".

242. *Aquélla*: "la luz divina".

244-6. *y, cual de amor . . . se cubrirá*: "y, cual la matutina estrella (i.e. Venus) . . . el alma se cubrirá de amor".

247. *la hermosísima judía*: Rachel. The reference is to *Genesis* xxiv, 64-5.

248. *doncel*: here, "virginal".

249. *que para sí venía*: "que venía hacia ella".

266. *las musas de Dios*: i.e. the angels.

285. *del cretense padre el hijo insano*: Icarus, the son of Daedalus, the inventor of the Cretan labyrinth, who flew too near the sun and was destroyed.

289. *de Pindo las hermanas nueve*: The muses leave Mt. Pindus, their traditional home, to dwell on Mt. Sion (l. 292). Probably an allusion to Montano's Latin poems, in which Christian doctrine is expressed in classical forms.

299. *Aldino*: Aldana's pastoral pseudonym for himself. (Cf. l. 442.)

312. *casi*: "como". (Cf. l. 401.)

318. *ensayo*: here, "prueba, peso".

330. *con lo demás*: with the other deadly sins, anger and gluttony. *El padre antiguo*: Adam.

337. *Anteo*: Antaeus, the giant whom Hercules fought as one of his seven labours. He gained new strength each time he touched the earth, his mother; Hercules finally strangled him by lifting him in the air (cf. l. 341). In the allegory which follows, Antaeus represents the body and Hercules the soul.

342. *porque el favor no pase della en éste*: "para que ninguna fuerza nueva se transmita de la tierra *(della)* al cuerpo rebelde *(ese imperfeto)*".

343. *tanto que el pie del sensitivo afe(c)to*: until the senses, like the feet of Antaeus, lose contact with earth.

346. *de sí le apartará*: "el alma apartará el cuerpo *(el enemigo)* de sí".

349-51. *serán temor de Dios . . . de toda esencia*: The sense of these lines is not clear. I would suggest: "Las fuerzas *(los brazos)* con que el alma domará el cuerpo serán el temor de Dios, y la penitencia; (mientras que) la caridad (será) coronada de diadema (y) el valor (será coronado) de toda esencia".

352 etc. The natural description which follows was probably suggested by Monte Urgull, the site of the fortress of San Sebastián. (See biographical note.)

367. *dos elementos*: the sea and the land.

378. *lucillas*: "lucirlas".

383. *bucíos*: probably "buccinos".

402. *reparador*: "protector".

405. *puro*: "indefenso".

423. *Carón*: Charon, the boatman who ferried the dead across the river Styx.

425. *que por sirena nos figura:* "que la antigüedad solía representar bajo la forma de una sirena". What follows is a rationalization of the myth of the Sirens.

431–2. *aun despierto . . . le desfallece:* This refers back to *marinero* (l. 428).

446–7. *que nunca . . . pueda.* Aldana argues that Montano is the whole, of which he himself is a part: "que nunca me separe yo *(esta tu parte)* de ti *(su todo)* y que siempre pueda ser parte tuya".

Mira, Filis, furiosa (p. 126)

25. *al errante y fijo coro:* the fixed and moving stars.

Sigo, silencio, tu estrello manto (p. 127)

3–4. *enemiga del Sol . . . ave nocturna:* the poet identifies himself with the *ave nocturna*, presumably the owl.

¿ Adónde te escondiste (p. 134)

(Quotations from the prose commentary are indicated by the abbreviation *CE.*)

San Juan summarizes the argument of the poem as follows: "El orden que llevan estas canciones es desde que un alma comienza a servir a Dios hasta que llega a un último estado de perfección que es matrimonio espiritual, y así en ellas se tocan los tres estados o vías de ejercicio espiritual por las cuales pasa el alma hasta llegar al dichoso estado, que son: purgativa, iluminativa y unitiva, y se declaran acerca de cada una algunas propiedades y efectos della" *(CE, Argumento).* The basic allegory of the poem, which describes the spiritual marriage of Christ and the soul, is founded on the traditional Christian interpretation of the *Song of Solomon*. In terms of the allegory, the three stages referred to above correspond to the search (ll. 1–60), the encounter (ll. 61–135) and the marriage (ll. 136–200). In the two earliest texts of the poem, the Sanlúcar and the Jaén manuscripts, a number of stanzas appear in a different order. Cf. Dámaso Alonso: "en la primera ordenación, la de Sanlúcar (the text which is printed here), el alma, con un impulso irresistible, se adelanta hacia la unión, estado en que le sobrevienen todavía recelos y temores; en la segunda (la de Jaén), el proceso purificativo es más perfecto y la posesión ya no perturbada".

15. *los fuertes:* "A los demonios . . . llama fuertes, porque ellos con gran fuerza procuran tomar el paso de este camino" *(CE).*

27. *de vero:* "de veras". This line is addressed to the soul, the next line to the *Esposo.*

31. *Y todos cuantos vagan:* "Y todos los que sirven a Dios". These are the "rational creatures" (angels and men), as distinct from the "irrational creatures" *(bosques . . . espesuras . . . prado)* addressed in ll. 16–20.

35. *un no sé qué que quedan balbuciendo:* "si lo otro que entiendo me llaga y hiere

de amor, esto que no acabo de entender, de que altamente siento, me mata"
(CE). Notice the extraordinary onomatopoeic effect of this line.

36–7. *¿cómo perseveras . . . donde vives:* "¿cómo puedes perseverar en el cuerpo
. . . ?" *(CE)*.

38–40. *y haciendo . . . concibes?:* "y puesto que te matan las flechas que recibes
del concepto del Amado que tienes dentro de ti".

41. *has llagado:* addressed to the *Esposo*.

54. *que:* The second *que*, though grammatically redundant, gives a flavour
of popular speech. This stanza is not included in the Sanlúcar manuscript.
It is stanza 11 in the Jaén manuscript, and appears in the Rome edition of
1627, which otherwise follows the Sanlúcar version.

56. *¡Oh cristalina fuente:* The "fount" stands for faith. Cf. *John* iv, 14: "who-
soever drinketh of the water that I shall give him shall never have thirst".

61–2. *Apártalos, Amado, / que voy de vuelo:* At this point the soul's search comes
to an end; but it cannot bear the divine gaze while it is still joined to the
body. Cf. "que voy de vuelo de la carne, para que me lo comuniques (i.e.
'el espíritu divino') fuera della, siendo ellos (los ojos del Amado) la causa
de hacerme volar de la carne" *(CE)*.

63. *Vuélvete, paloma:* The *Esposo* restrains the soul; it is not yet time for it to
leave the body. (The soul is also like the dove which flies back to the Ark,
the symbol of divine charity.) He now offers himself to the soul's contem-
plation in the form of a wounded deer: "si llagado vas de amor de mí, yo
también como el ciervo vengo, en esta tu llaga llagado, a ti" *(CE)*.

67. *nemorosos:* "umbríos".

77. *cuevas de leones:* The soul, in its union with Christ, is protected from the
passións, as the lions' caves are secure against other animals.

82. *las jóvenes:* "Es a saber, las almas devotas, con fuerzas de juventud recibidas
de la realidad de tu huella" *(CE)*.

86–7. *En la interior bodega / de mi Amado bebí:* "En la interior bodega (de mi
alma) bebí de mi Amado". The innermost part of the soul is a receptacle
for the *adorado vino* "(que) se difunde y derrama por todos los miembros y
venas del cuerpo" *(CE)*.

90. *y el ganado perdí:* "Es de saber, que hasta que el alma llegue a este estado de
perfección de que vamos hablando, aunque más espiritual sea, siempre le
queda algún ganadillo de apetitos y gustillos y otras imperfecciones suyas"
(CE). Cf. also l. 98.

101. *ejido:* "un lugar común donde la gente se suele juntar a tomar solaz y
recreación; y donde también los pastores apacientan sus ganados; y así por
el ejido entiende aquí el alma el mundo" *(CE)*.

115. *y en uno de mis ojos te llagaste:* "Entiéndese aquí por el ojo la fe, y dice uno
solo, y que en él se llagó, porque si la fe y fidelidad del alma para con Dios
no fuese sola, sino que estuviese mezclada con otro algún respecto o cumpli-
miento, no llegaría a efecto de llagar a Dios de amor. Y así sólo un ojo ha de
ser en que se llaga, como también un solo cabello en que se prenda el
Amado" *(CE)*.

118. *adamabas:* "enamorabas". There is a strong current of popular, rustic vocabulary in this and other poems by San Juan. Cf. *ejido, majadas, compañas, montiña, manidas* (in *Aunque es de noche*).

126. *Cazadnos:* addressed to the angels.

130. *y no parezca nadie en la montiña:* "y que no aparezca nadie en la montaña'. Cf. note to l. 118.

132. *recuerdas:* "despiertas".

141. *Debajo del manzano:* In medieval symbology, the tree in Eden is a proto-type of the Cross. *Tu madre* (l. 145) is human nature.

152–3. *y canto de serenas os conjuro, / que cesen vuestras iras: serenas* = "sirenas". *Os* refers to *aves ligeras* etc.: these represent the various powers which distract the soul. *Muro* (l. 154) is the "wall" which peace and virtue erect around the soul.

156. *ninfas de Judea:* In *CE*, these represent the fantasies of the imagination, which are sensuous *(ninfas)* and capricious, like the Jews in their relations with God. On the same analogy, *los arrabales* (l. 159) refers to the sensitive part of the soul, which is a prey to imagination.

161. *Escóndete:* "Como si dijera: Querido Esposo mío, recógete en lo más interior de mi alma, comunicándote a ella escondidamente, manifestándole tus escondidas maravillas, ajenas de todos los ojos mortales" *(CE)*. *Las montañas,* in *CE,* refers to the powers of the soul: memory, understanding and will.

163. *y no quieras decillo:* "do not speak to the soul through the senses, as before, but work in it directly and silently".

164–5. *las compañas . . . ínsulas extrañas:* "compañas son la multitud de virtudes y dones y perfecciones y otras riquezas espirituales que (Dios) ha puesto ya en ella". Here, as elsewhere, *ínsulas* suggests the journey of the soul through "vías extrañas y ajenas de todos los sentidos y del común conocimiento natural" *(CE)*.

166. *la blanca palomica:* Cf. l. 63: *Vuélvete paloma,* where the dove returning to the Ark after its first, unsuccessful, flight suggested the imperfect situation of the soul, whose complete union with Christ is now symbolized by the dove returning with the olive-branch.

168. *la tortolica:* In *CE,* San Juan paraphrases part of the well-known *Romance de Fontefrida:* "es de saber que de la tortolica se escribe que cuando ya halla al consorte, ni se asienta en ramo verde, ni bebe el agua ni clara ni fría, ni se pone debajo de la sombra, ni se junta con otras aves". (Cf. note to ll. 191–3.)

169. *socio:* "consorte".

176. *Gocémonos, amado:* At this point in the poem, the soul, which has now reached the highest degree of union which is possible in this life, speculates on the still deeper knowledge of God which it may enjoy in eternity. The change of tense *(mostrarías . . . darías)* emphasizes the difference.

181–2. *las subidas / cavernas de la piedra:* "la piedra que aquí dice, según dice San Pablo *(I Cor.* 10), es Cristo. Las subidas cavernas de esta piedra son los subidos y altos y profundos misterios de la sabiduría de Dios, que hay en Cristo" *(CE)*.

185. *granadas*: "Porque así como las granadas tienen muchos granicos nacidos y sustentados en aquel seno circular, así cada uno de los atributos y misterios y juicios y virtudes de Dios contiene en sí gran multitud de ordenaciones maravillosas y admirables efectos de Dios, contenidos y sustentados en el seno esférico de virtud y misterio, etc." *(CE)*

191–3. *El aspirar del aire . . . y su donaire*: This seems a clear reminiscence of Garcilaso, Second Eclogue, ll. 1146–53, which also refer to the turtle-dove (cf. l. 168): "el viento expira, / Filomena sospira en dulce canto, / y en amoroso llanto se amancilla; / gime la tortolilla sobre el ramo, / preséntanos a colmo el prado flores, / y esmalta en mil colores su verdura; / la fuente clara y pura murmurando / nos está convidando a dulce trato".

197. *Aminadab*: the devil. Cf. *Solomon* vi, 12.

196–200. The general sense of the final stanza is that the soul can now aspire to the deepest knowledge of God because all external movements and distractions have come to an end. *Cerco* refers to the passions and appetites which lay siege to the soul; *las aguas* are the waters of the spirit; *la caballería* represents the bodily senses, which join in the spiritual union as far as they are able. This is why they only "see" the water, without tasting it; only pure spirit can reach the essence of spiritual good; the senses know it indirectly, "por cierta redundancia ('overflowing') del espíritu" *(CE)*.

En una noche oscura (p. 140)

San Juan wrote two separate commentaries on this poem, *La subida del monte Carmelo* and *La noche oscura del alma*. The first, though it incorporates lines from the poem, is virtually an independent treatise; the second (referred to here as *NO*) keeps closer to the poem, but ends at line 11 *(En la noche dichosa)*.

1–10. "En las dos primeras canciones (i.e. "estrofas") se declaran los efectos de las dos purgaciones espirituales: de la parte sensitiva del hombre y de la espiritual" *(NO. Prólogo)*. The symbol of the "dark night of the soul", with its necessary complement, the "flame" of divine love, forms the core of San Juan's account of mystical experience. Here, the first stanza describes the "night of the senses" and the second the "night of the spirit", the two essential stages in the preparation of the soul for union with God.

5. *mi casa*: "la casa de la sensualidad . . . esto es, mortificadas sus pasiones, apagadas sus codicias, y los apetitos sosegados y adormidos por medio de esta noche dichosa de la purgación sensitiva" *(NO)*.

7. *por la secreta escala, disfrazada*: the ladder of contemplation by which the soul climbs to God. In *NO*, San Juan explains that the soul is disguised *(disfrazada)* in the colours of the three theological virtues: white, green and purple, standing respectively for faith, hope and charity.

19. *quien yo bien me sabía*: Christ ("el Esposo").

21. *¡ Oh noche que guiaste !*: The soul, now united with Christ *(amada en el amado transformada)*, looks back on its journey.

26–40. The last three stanzas, like the *Cántico espiritual*, reflect the tone and imagery of the *Song of Solomon*, though the amount of direct textual resemblance is slight. (*Cedros* and *almena* may have been suggested by *Solomon* viii, 9–10.) Notice the concentrated sequence of actions and the magnificent control of sound and rhythm in the final stanza (*Quedéme . . . olvidéme . . . recliné . . . dejéme,* / *dejando . . .*) as the soul lapses into oblivion.

¡ Oh llama de amor viva (p. 142)

In the prologue to *Llama de amor viva* (referred to here as *LA*), San Juan describes the transformation of the soul in one of his finest metaphors: "pero puede con el tiempo y ejercicio calificarse . . . y sustanciarse mucho más en el amor; bien así como aunque habiendo entrado el fuego en el madero le tenga transformado en sí y éste ya unido con él, todavía, afervorándose más el fuego y dando más tiempo en él se pone mucho más candente e inflamado hasta centellear fuego de sí y llamear".

6. *la tela:* the obstacle which divides the soul from God. In *LA*, San Juan describes three kinds of obstacle: temporal, natural and sensual.

7. *¡ Oh cauterio süave!:* "con ser este fuego de Dios tan vehemente y consumidor que con mayor facilidad consumiría mil mundos que el fuego una raspa de lino, no consuma o acabe los espíritus en que arde, sino que a la medida de su fuerza y ardor los deleite y endiose, ardiendo en ellos suavemente por la fuerza de sus espíritus" (*LA*).

13. *¡ Oh lámparas de fuego:* San Juan emphasizes the two properties of fire: burning (stanza 1) and giving light (stanza 3). This is close to *Solomon* viii, 6, which in the Vulgate reads: "lampades ejus, lampades ignis atque flammarum". (Cf. also l. 18: *calor y luz.*)

15. *las profundas cavernas del sentido: sentido* here means "sentido espiritual", "capacidad del alma para lo divino" (*LA*), the *más profundo centro del alma* of l. 3. The cavern image appears in *Solomon* ii, 14 ("In foraminibus petrae, in caverna maceriae") and is used in the *Cántico espiritual.* ll. 181–2. In *LA*, San Juan imagines the *profundo centro* as a well at the meeting-point of three caves, each corresponding to a faculty of the soul: understanding, will and memory. Each cave is purified in turn by the torches, the "lámparas divinas", so that it reflects heat and light back to their source in God. What makes the caves so effective as a poetic symbol is that they are neither concrete nor abstract, but "cavernas del sentido espiritual", capable of *feeling* their own transformation.

20. *recuerdas:* "es el recuerdo que haces". "En este recuerdo que el esposo hace en esta alma perfecta, todo es perfecto; porque él lo hace todo, y entonces en aquel excitar y recordar, que es al modo de como cuando uno recuerda y respira, siente el alma la aspiración de Dios" (*LA*).

Que bien sé yo la fonte que mana y corre (p. 143)

This is one of the poems which San Juan is thought to have composed during his imprisonment in Toledo. Night, here, is a metaphor for the soul's imprisonment in the body; it does not yet have the complex associations of *La noche oscura*. The refrain insists on the contrast between the confusion of the senses and the certainty of faith: *Que bien sé yo . . . aunque es de noche.*

1–2. The opening phrase *(Que bien . . .)* and the dialect form *fonte* for "fuente" suggest that this two-line theme may have been of popular origin. In a three-line *villancico, fonte* would have been necessary for the assonance in o—e: *fonte—corre—noche.*

13. *vadealla:* "vadearla".

24. *de estas dos:* The *fuente* is God the Father, from whom the other two persons of the Trinity issue as streams. *Estas dos* refers to *corriente* and *fuente* (l. 21); the second *corriente* is the remaining person of the Trinity, who is co-equal with the others *(que ninguna de ellas le precede).*

28. *este vivo pan:* the Eucharist.

Tras de un amoroso lance (p. 144)

Hawking imagery is common in secular love poetry of the sixteenth century. (For examples from Gil Vicente and Cetina, see pp. 16 and 70.) It also appears in *a lo divino* poetry in the second half of the century, and there are precedents in the religious prose of Francisco de Osuna (d. bef. 1542) and other writers. Three anonymous poems have been suggested as direct precedents for San Juan's poem (see Dámaso Alonso, *Boletín de la Real Academia Española*, xxvi, 1947, pp. 63–79, reprinted in *De los siglos oscuros al de Oro*, Gredos, Madrid, 1958); the closest appears in a manuscript in the Biblioteca Nacional, Madrid, and begins: "Tras de un amoroso lance, / aunque de esperanzas falto, / subí tan alto, tan alto, / que le di a la caza alcance". It is likely that this represents the primitive version of the lines glossed by San Juan; notice the significant change of sense in the second line.

1. *lance:* "búsqueda, caza".

26. *Y abatíme tanto, tanto:* Though there are other parallels in earlier mystical writing, it has been suggested that San Juan found the source of this paradox in an anonymous poem published in the *Floresta de varia poesía* of Diego Ramírez de Pagán (1562). The passage in question reads: "El sacre que la seguía (i.e. 'el halcón que seguía a la garza') / si con vuelo muy ligero / se encumbraba, / cuanto más alto subía, / tanto más bajo y rastrero / se quedaba".

Un pastorcico solo está penado (p. 145)

Apart from the final stanza, this poem is modelled on an anonymous pastoral poem in *redondillas*, recently discovered by Blecua in a manuscript in the Bibliothèque Nationale, Paris, and reprinted by Dámaso Alonso in *Poesía española*, Madrid, 1950, p. 257. San Juan has transformed a slight pastoral lament into an intense allegory of the Redemption.

3. *su pastora*: the human soul.

11. *en tierra ajena*: the earth itself, where Christ is ill-treated by men.

14. *de aquel que de mi amor ha hecho ausencia*: "Woe to him (Satan) who has made my love forget me".

18. *sobre un árbol*: the Cross. Cf. 1 *Peter* ii, 21, 23–5, a passage which San Juan may have had in mind when composing this poem: "Christ who suffered for us . . . Who His own self bare our sins in His own body on the tree .·. . For ye were as sheep going astray; but are now returned unto the Shepherd and Bishop of your souls".

GLOSSARY

This list contains only rare and archaic forms not mentioned in the notes to the poems.

aborrir aborrecer
adó adonde
aferes negocios
agora, ora ahora
amostrar mostrar
ansí así
asconder esconder

basquillas basquiñas
broslar bordar

cabelladura cabellera
(en) cas de en casa de
cativo cautivo
complida cumplida
contino, de contino continuo, continuamente
convertilda convertidla
cualque alguno
cubijadas cubiertas

decendiese desciendiese
defeto defecto
dende desde
dino, indino, indinación digno, indigno, indignación

ecelsa excelsa
efeto efecto
ejorcas ajorcas
encomendedes encomendéis
escuro, escuridad, escurecer obscuro, obscuridad, obscurecer
esparnancadas esparrancadas
estó estoy

felice feliz
finarse morirse
fuemos fuimos
fuerdes fuereis

gelos, ge los se los
guardedes guardéis

haberá habrá
hane han
haz faz
hecistes hicistes

interese interés
interrompa interrumpa
ivierno invierno

levar llevar

mesmo mismo
mesquina mezquina
mochacha muchacha
morá morad

namorar enamorar
nemorosos umbríos
nesta en esta
non no
nublado anublado

oyas oigas

pece pez
perfición perfección

questos aquestos, estos

repuno repugno

salce, sauz sauce
sepoltura sepultura
só soy
sospirar suspirar
sotil sutil
süez soez

ternás tendrás
travesar atravesar
trayo traigo

vernán vendrán
ves: tan mala ves: vez; apenas, dificultosamente
vevir vivir
vía veía
vido vio
vidro vidrio
vierdes viereis
virgo virgen
vitoria victoria
vo voy

SUGGESTIONS
FOR FURTHER READING

For reasons of space, this list only includes books. Some of the best criticism of sixteenth-century poetry has appeared in the form of articles in periodicals; many of these are referred to in the studies and editions listed here and in the notes on individual poets. Readers may also consult *The Year's Work in Modern Language Studies*, published annually by the Modern Humanities Research Association (Cambridge University Press) and the check-lists contained in *Publications of the Modern Language Association of America (PMLA)*.

ANTHOLOGIES

D. Alonso, *Poesía de la Edad Media y poesía de tipo tradicional*, Losada, Buenos Aires 1942.

D. Alonso and J. M. Blecua, *Antología de la poesía española: poesía de tipo tradicional*, Gredos, Madrid, 1956.

GENERAL STUDIES

M. Menéndez Pelayo, *Antología de poetas líricos castellanos*, Consejo Superior de Investigaciones Científicas, Madrid, 1944–5, 10 vols.; Vol. III *(cancionero* poets, Encina, Gil Vicente). (Vol. IV contains an anthology of these poets.)

R. Menéndez Pidal, *Romancero hispánico*, Espasa-Calpe, Madrid, 1953, 2 vols.

P. Le Gentil, *La poésie espagnole et portugaise à la fin du moyen âge*, Plihon, Rennes, 1949–53, 2 vols. *(cancionero* poetry).

M. Frenk Alatorre, *La lírica popular en los siglos de oro*, Mexico, 1946.

P. Salinas, *Jorge Manrique, o tradición y originalidad*, Ed. Sudamericana, Buenos Aires, 1947 *(cancionero* poetry).

B. W. Wardropper, *Historia de la poesía lírica a lo divino en la cristiandad occidental*, Revista de Occidente, Madrid, 1958.

F. W. Pierce, *La poesía épica del Siglo de Oro*, Gredos, Madrid, 1961; 2nd ed., revised 1968.

J. G. Fucilla, *Estudios sobre el petrarquismo en España*, Revista de Filología Española, Anejo 72, Madrid, 1960.

G. Díaz-Plaja (ed.), *Historia general de las literaturas hispánicas* Vol. II, Ed. Barna, Barcelona, 1951 (includes essays on *romances*, *cancionero* and Italianate poetry, Herrera).

G. Díaz-Plaja, *Historia de la poesía lírica española*, 2nd ed., Labor, Barcelona, 1948.

STUDIES OF INDIVIDUAL POETS

P. GALLAGHER, *The Life and Works of Garci Sánchez de Badajoz*, Támesis, London, 1968.

J. M. COSSÍO, *Fábulas mitológicas en España*, Espasa-Calpe, Madrid, 1952. (Castillejo)

M. MENÉNDEZ PELAYO, *Antología* (see above), Vol X. (Boscán)

M. ARCE BLANCO, *Garcilaso de la Vega*, Revista de Filología Española, Anejo 13, Madrid, 1930.

H. KENISTON, *Garcilaso de la Vega*, Hispanic Society of New York, 1922.

R. LAPESA, *La trayectoria poética de Garcilaso*, Revista de Occidente, Madrid, 1948.

A. GALLEGO MORELL, *Dos ensayos sobre poesía española del siglo XVI*, Ínsula, Madrid, 1951. (Garcilaso, Hurtado de Mendoza, Cetina, Acuña, Herrera)

D. ALONSO, *Poesía española*, Gredos, Madrid, 1950; 2nd. ed., revised, with index, 1952. (Garcilaso, Luis de León, San Juan de la Cruz)

P. SALINAS, *Reality and the poet in Spanish poetry*, Johns Hopkins Press, Baltimore, 1940. (Garcilaso, Luis de León, San Juan de la Cruz)

M. BATAILLON, *Erasmo en España*, Fondo de cultura económica, Mexico, 1950, 2 vols, (Montemayor)

A. MARÍN OCETE, *Gregorio Silvestre*, Madrid, 1939.

A. F. G. BELL, *Luis de León*, Clarendon Press, Oxford, 1925.

K. VOSSLER, *Luis de León*, Austral. no. 565, Espasa-Calpe, Buenos Aires, 1946.

A. COSTER, *Fernando de Herrera*, Champion, Paris, 1908.

O. MACRÍ, *Fernando de Herrera*, Gredos, Madrid, 1959.

E. L. RIVERS, *Francisco de Aldana*, Institución de servicios culturales, Badajoz, 1955.

D. ALONSO, *La poesía de San Juan de la Cruz*, Consejo Superior de Investigaciones Científicas, Madrid, 1942; 2nd. ed., Aguilar (Crisol), Madrid, 1946 (with text of poems and selections from prose commentaries); 3rd. ed., Aguilar (Ensayistas hispánicas), Madrid, 1958.

J. GUILLÉN, *Language and poetry*, Harvard U.P., Cambridge, Mass., 1961. (San Juan de la Cruz) Spanish edition: *Lenguaje y poesía*, Revista de Occidente, Madrid, 1962.

INDEX OF FIRST LINES

A Dafne ya los brazos le crecían (GARCILASO)   44
¿Adónde te escondiste (SAN JUAN)   134
Ahí van las ansias mías (BOSCÁN)   37
Ahora que cubrió de blanco hielo (HERRERA)   103
Alma, que ya en la luz del puro cielo (HERRERA)   102
Alma región luciente (LUIS DE LEÓN)   93
Amor, en un incendio no acabado (HERRERA)   103
Amor, no me dejes (ALVAREZ GATO)   9
Antigua llaga que en mis huesos cría (BOSCÁN)   37
Aquella voluntad honesta y pura (GARCILASO)   47
Como aquel que en soñar gusto recibe (BOSCÁN)   39
Como el patrón, que en golfo navegando (BOSCÁN)   39
Como garza real, alta en el cielo (CETINA)   70
Como vemos que un río mansamente (ACUÑA)   68
Con un manso rüido (GARCILASO)   45
Cual simple mariposa vuelve al fuego (D. HURTADO DE
    MENDOZA)   62
Cuando contemplo el cielo (LUIS DE LEÓN)   90
Cuando la brava ausencia un alma hiere (GIL POLO)   131
¡Cuántas veces te he has engalanado (F. DE LA TORRE)   128
De dentro tengo mi mal (CAMOENS)   81
Decid los que tratáis de agricultura (SILVESTRE)   72
Dicen que me case yo (GIL VICENTE)   17
Dulce el fuego de Amor, dulce la pena (HERRERA)   102
Dulce soñar y dulce congojarme (BOSCÁN)   38
El aire se serena (LUIS DE LEÓN)   89
¡El mi corazón, madre (FERNÁNDEZ DE HEREDIA)   20
El vaso reluciente y cristalino (CAMOENS)   83
En el placiente verano (XIMÉNEZ DE URREA)   5
En fin, en fin, tras tanto andar muriendo (ALDANA)   112
En la huerta nace la rosa (GIL VICENTE)   16
En mí cría, Señor, corazón limpio (MONTEMAYOR)   78
En tanto que de rosa y azucena (GARCILASO)   44
En una noche oscura (SAN JUAN)   140
Enemiga le soy, madre (FERNÁNDEZ DE HEREDIA)   21
Escrito está en mi alma vuestro gesto (GARCILASO)   43
Halcón que se atreve (GIL VICENTE)   16
Hola, gentil Galatea (CASTILLEJO)   23
Horas alegres que pasáis volando (CETINA)   71

Id, suspiros ardientes (ALCÁZAR)	96
Irme quiero, madre (CAMOENS)	82
La mucha tristeza mía (GARCI SÁNCHEZ)	1
La vida se nos pasa, el tiempo vuela (SILVESTRE)	73
Los amores de la niña (GIL VICENTE)	18
Madre, cuando enviudaré (XIMÉNEZ DE URREA)	6
Memorias tristes del placer pasado (LAYNEZ)	130
Mil veces callo que romper deseo (ALDANA)	112
Mira, Filis, furiosa (F. DE LA TORRE)	126
Montano, cuyo nombre es la primera (ALDANA)	113
Mortales: habéis visto mayor cosa (SILVESTRE)	73
Muy graciosa es la doncella (GIL VICENTE)	15
Nadie fíe en alegría (D. HURTADO DE MENDOZA)	61
No bañes en el mar sagrado y cano (HERRERA)	99
No la debemos dormir (FRAY A. MONTESINO)	10
No pueden dormir mis ojos (CASTILLEJO)	23
No te tardes que me muero (ENCINA)	12
¡O gran fuerza de amor, que así enflaqueces (BOSCÁN)	38
¡Oh llama de amor viva (SAN JUAN)	142
Ojos claros, serenos (CETINA)	69
Ojos garzos ha la niña (ENCINA)	11
Partiendo de la luz, donde solía (FIGUEROA)	109
Por unos puertos arriba (ENCINA)	13
Por vos ardí, señora, y por vos ardo (CETINA)	70
Que bien sé yo la fonte que mana y corre (SAN JUAN)	143
¡Qué descansada vida (LUIS DE LEÓN)	86
Que las manos tengo blandas (FERNÁNDEZ DE HEREDIA)	20
Quien ve las blancas y hermosas rosas (FIGUEROA)	110
¡Quién viese aquel día (SÁ DE MIRANDA)	40
Rasga la venda y mira lo que haces (ALCÁZAR)	97
Rojo sol, que con hacha luminosa (1582 version) (HERRERA)	104
Rojo sol, que con hacha luminosa (1619 version) (HERRERA)	105
Rojo sol, que con llama glorïosa (1578 version) (HERRERA)	104
Salga con la doliente ánima fuera (LAYNEZ)	129
¡Sea bienvenido, sea (MONTEMAYOR)	80
Secáronme los pesares (GARCI SÁNCHEZ)	4
Señor Gómez Arias (HOROZCO)	63
Sigo, silencio, tu estrellado manto (F. DE LA TORRE)	127
¡Sola me dejaste (SÁ DE MIRANDA)	41
Soy garridica (TIMONEDA)	75
Tras de un amoroso lance (SAN JUAN)	144
Tres serranas he encontrado (TIMONEDA)	76
Tu gracia, tu valor, tu hermosura (D. HURTADO DE MENDOZA)	62
Un novillo feroz y un fuerte toro (ACUÑA)	67

Un pastorcico solo está penado (SAN JUAN) 145
Va y viene mi pensamiento (D. HURTADO DE MENDOZA) 59
Vanse mis amores, madre (GIL VICENTE) 18
Véante mis ojos (SANTA TERESA) 65
Venida es, venida (ALVAREZ GATO) 8
Voz de dolor y canto de gemido (HERRERA) 105
Vuela y cerca la lumbre y no reposa (HERRERA) 101
¡Y dejas, Pastor santo (LUIS DE LEÓN) 94
Ya de mis quietos días el sereno (LOMAS CANTORAL) 84